PROPERTY OF
P9-BYX-737

"As for our definition of "the South".... We've included the easy ones: the Carolinas, Tennessee, Georgia, Alabama, Mississippi and Arkansas. Also Louisiana, although it complicates our discussion of everything from food to religion. Virginia for historical reasons, if nothing else. And the rest of the former Confederacy: the states of Texas and Florida and the territory of Oklahoma. Kentucky's in here, too. A state known for fast horses, bourbon whiskey and fried chicken just can't be left out of the South."

1001 Things Everyone Should Know About the South,
John Shelton Reed and Dale Volberg Reed, 1996

"The South is a place.
East, west and north are nothing but directions."

Richmond Times-Dispatch, 1995

Southern Divorce

The southern way of divorce as well as specific family law information for Florida, Georgia, the Carolinas, Virginia, Tennessee, Kentucky, Mississippi, Louisiana, Arkansas and Oklahoma

John C. Mayoue

Published by PSG Books
Dallas, Texas

Southern Divorce
John C. Mayoue

PSG Books
9603 White Rock Trail, Suite 310   Dallas, Texas 75238
214/340-6223   214/340-6209 fax
acquisitions@psgbooks.com

Copyright 2004 by John C. Mayoue and Professional Solutions Group

All rights reserved. No part of this book may be reproduced or trans-mitted in any form by any means, electronic, mechanical, photocopy-ing, recording or otherwise, without the prior written permission of the publisher. The only exceptions to this rule are for brief quotations in critical reviews or articles.

Books published under the imprint of PSG Books are distributed to the U.S. book trade by Independent Publishers' Group, 814 N. Franklin St., Chicago, Illinois 60610 and can be ordered by calling 1-800-888-4741. Resellers outside the book trade who wish to purchase books in quan-tity at a discount may contact PSG Books at 1-800-465-1508.

Attorney and author John C. Mayoue is available to speak to groups on the subject of divorce. He can be reached at 3350 Riverwood Parkway, Suite 2300, Atlanta, GA 30339, 770-951-2700 (voice), 770-951-2200 (fax), e-mail: Jmayoue@wmbnclaw.com.

ISBN 0-9659273-5-0

Manufactured in the United States of America

9 8 7 6 5 4 3 2 1

Library of Congress Cataloging-in-Publication Data

Mayoue, John C., 1954-
Southern divorce / John C. Mayoue.
      p. cm.
      Subtitle: Southern trends in divorce as well as specific family law information for Florida, Georgia, the Carolinas, Virginia, Tennessee, Kentucky, Mississippi, Louisiana, Arkansas, and Oklahoma.
      ISBN 0-9659273-5-0
      1. Divorce--Law and legislation--Southern States--Popular works. 2. Divorce suits--Southern States--Popular works. 3. Domestic relations--Southern States--Popular works. I. Title.

      KF535.Z9M29 2004
      346.7501'66--dc22

                                    2004014918

NOTICE AND DISCLAIMER

State laws, legal precedents and regulations vary greatly from one jurisdiction to another and change over time. Because of these variations, the reader should not use this book for specific legal advice. Every divorce case and post-divorce action is unique, requiring the advice of those versed in the laws of the jurisdiction where the action is taken.

This book is intended to provide readers with a general overview of matters related to the divorce process and post-divorce issues, so they may take legal action or otherwise address these issues better informed.

Consult an attorney for specific information related to your personal situation.

ABOUT THE AUTHOR

John C. Mayoue is one of the best-known divorce attorneys in the South. His clients have included Marianne Gingrich, ex-wife of former House Speaker Newt Gingrich; actress Jane Fonda, communications mogul Ted Turner's ex; baseball star David Justice, former husband of actress Halle Berry; Janice Holyfield, former wife of heavyweight boxing champion Evander Holyfield; and Marianne Rogers, ex-wife of country singer Kenny Rogers.

One of his most famous cases was that of "Baby Gregory." The baby's parents were accused of abuse by Tennessee officials after they abducted him and took him to a children's hospital in Atlanta. Later, Mayoue and one of his law partners won a ruling that the parents' actions were in the best interest of the child and that Baby Gregory belonged with them.

Mayoue attended Transylvania University in Kentucky and Emory School of Law in Atlanta. He decided to live in Atlanta after graduation.

Mayoue specialized in divorce litigation because of the profound effect it has on people. "Here you're dealing with something that's real," he says. "There's emotion attached to it. Real, live people need help and you can give it."

Mayoue is the author of *Balancing Competing Interests in Family Law* published by the Family Law Section of the American Bar Association. He speaks to business and professional groups and is available to speak to civic and parent groups on the various facets of family law.

Publisher

FOREWORD BY "DREAM TEAM" ATTORNEY JOHNNIE COCHRAN

The modern South described by John Mayoue is very different from the South I knew as a boy. I spoke of that region in my first book, *Journey to Justice,* and of my roots that "…run through the rich, black earth of my family's love, across the continent and back nearly sixty years to a clapboard house on a red dirt hill in Shreveport, Louisiana, and to the Little Union Baptist Church where I first heard the voices that have been with me ever since…."

Divorce was unheard of in the South of my boyhood. It was a region so indelibly connected to family that I couldn't imagine all of us not being together. But with the passage of time, the South has become more like the rest of the country, with problems that affect us all.

For a divorce attorney like Mayoue, those problems include the dissolution of families at an alarming rate. I have worked with Mayoue on some precedent-setting court cases. I recognize him as an extraordinary man of integrity as well as a creative legal mind who does what he does to help people.

He is ideally suited to produce a book that combines sociological insights with common sense solutions to the problem of divorce.

Both Mayoue and I approach the law from a global perspective. When I walk into a courtroom, I'm not merely defending the individual who stands accused. I'm defending a legal system that guarantees the presumption of innocence and every individual's right to equal protection under the law.

Mayoue enters the courtroom as an advocate for those he represents and many thousands of people he will never know but who are placing their futures on the line in the family court system. This book, *Southern Divorce,* is his way of helping those he does not represent. He offers them safe haven as well as saving them from their own passionate need to strike back for hurts that are real or imagined.

I cannot stop crime and corruption, but I can help derail attempts to further victimize everyone involved in the legal system. Mayoue cannot stop divorce, but he can help people emerge less battered and bruised by the process. Success at reducing the tensions associated with divorce is a worthwhile goal for the New South.

Johnnie L. Cochran, Jr.

Note: In the mid-1990s, Johnnie Cochran gained international recognition as lead attorney for the Dream Team that defended O.J. Simpson. Since then, Cochran has written two books, hosted a live weeknight talk show on Court TV and continues to practice law and court controversy. He and author John Mayoue have known each other for years and have a great deal of mutual respect.

INTRODUCTION

In a strict legal sense, there is no such thing as a southern divorce, although divorcing people throughout the region share many common values and have common experiences. Divorce is based on the statutes and controlling law of the individual states, not of the region or the nation. State laws determine the way family court actions proceed, and those actions can be vastly different from state to state. Whenever possible in this book, legal differences from one state to another are taken into account. There may be changes in the laws of those states between the time we write this and when you read it. We cannot be held responsible for those changes. But on several occasions in the book, we anticipate new laws or court interpretations of old ones.

From my law office in Atlanta, I have been fortunate to represent some of the nation's most famous and successful people. But this is not a tell-all book on celebrity divorce. I have a history of closed-mouth attendance to the privacy needs of these people, and that's one of the reasons they hire me. I happen to believe that all divorcing couples – rich or poor, famous or not – deserve privacy at a difficult time like this. References to cases and clients in this book contain real-life examples only where I have permission to use this information or it describes clients other than my own. Some examples are composites taken from my files and stories told to me by others.

Just as people are different from each other, so are the facts of each case. And the outcome of a case is dependent on the facts as well as the personalities involved. You may have a case with facts that sound much like those mentioned in one of our examples. This similarity is coincidental and does not ensure a similar outcome.

A word of caution. Do not use this book as a replacement for specific legal advice. It is not a how-to book on representing yourself.

This book is our attempt to educate and inform you about successfully divorcing in the South. To use an artistic analogy, these southern states are the canvas on which we create a scene of divorce. Successful divorce is the painting on that canvas. Use this book to complete that painting in vivid, pleasing colors that will make the rest of your life worth living.

John C. Mayoue

TABLE OF CONTENTS

The South is still around, for there are still Southerners, though most of us have decided upon our Southernness. And while in the age of glass office towers and jet travel and the cyberhalls of the Internet the South may exist more as memory than as fact, so long as it is remembered – or misremembered as myth – it will persist.

The Artificial Southerner
Reprinted with permission of the University of Arkansas Press. Copyright 2001 by Philip Martin.

PART ONE

Divorce: The Big Decision

Divorce In Numbers We Never Imagined

Who would have thought that people in the Bible Belt, the home of family values, would register the highest rates of divorce in the country? It is abundantly clear to family law specialists across the South that our courts are clogged with people splitting up. But who could have imagined the religious, economic and psychosocial reasoning behind this phenomenon without the extensive research that went into this book?

One by one, statistical analyses tell us what conventional wisdom says is impossible: Divorce is more rampant in the South than anywhere else in the country. Even in the new millennium, when divorce rates have begun to decrease in many parts of the country, rates in the South are still relatively high.

The story of divorce in the South mirrors the evolution of the region itself. The sleepy, antebellum Old South contrasts with the bustling, high-growth New South. Let's look at them both through the prism of divorce. In the Old South, divorce was almost non-existent. The New South developed in the 1970s, when as many as 65% of all marriages self-destructed. Moving into a new century, those rates have flattened considerably. But still, more than 350,000 divorces take place in the South each year. It is instructive to look at the many reasons why people in the New South divorce so frequently and what efforts are being made to stem this tide.

Examining the history and sociology behind this evolution allows us to offer a means of reducing the pain and despair that naturally accompanies divorce. This new trend in marital breakups is known as successful divorce or even, as improbable as it may sound, good divorce. The approach is a practical one, understanding that no one has the ability to control divorce.

Wherever families come together, they also break apart. But if you insist on divorcing, here's an approach that can allow you and your children to weather the storm and emerge emotionally and financially intact.

LOOKING AT DIVORCE
FROM ANOTHER PERSPECTIVE

Successful divorce contradicts the stereotype. For the most part, divorce is considered a mean-spirited, nasty action that must end happiness for everyone involved. The stereotype includes men strapped to the support wagon, while women are condemned to poverty and children to lives of underachievement.

Those who work in the courts see families go up in flames from anger and hurt each day, exhausting every last dollar they have rather than letting the other side extract a penny. Fueled by the need for revenge, these same clients use their children as psychological battering rams because they feel slighted or insulted by a soon-to-be ex-spouse. Formerly loving couples eviscerate each other just to see the other one bleed. Our alternative isn't a divorce guaranteed to make you happy. No one is naïve about this process. Divorce is hell for the vast majority of people, but it doesn't have to destroy you. With a successful divorce, you can emerge from the process safe and sane. People can rebuild their lives. Children do not have to be scarred for life, lacking in self esteem.

This book doesn't tackle the daunting question of how to reduce the divorce rate in the southern states which include, for our purposes, Florida, Georgia, the Carolinas, Virginia, Tennessee, Kentucky, Mississippi, Louisiana, Arkansas and Oklahoma.

The only states of the Old South not specifically targeted are Alabama and Texas, although we offer examples that originate from those states. The publisher, PSG Books, already has several fine books written specifically to the laws of those states, and they are mentioned on the back page of this book. Although Oklahoma is not usually thought of as a state of the Old South, the efforts of politicians and religious figures in that state to combat divorce resemble those of its more southern neighbors.

Successful Divorce
The Primary Goal

It is entirely possible to embrace a civilized version of divorce, one fed by common sense rather than ego or raw passion. A successful divorce takes the teamwork of attorney, client, family and friends working in the same direction.

Divorce in this context is not some soft approach to letting the other side push you around for the sake of keeping the peace. It has a fair and equitable result arrived at in a sane, intelligent manner. Sometimes it demands toughness, at other times compromise. A successful divorce is a process of getting to "yes" so people can move their lives forward constructively. A successful southern divorce is one that emphasizes fairness in family dissolution under the unique strictures of the Bible Belt.

2

Our New Southern Tradition

Divorce was not an option for the Rev. Charles Stanley, even during the darkest days of his marriage. As senior pastor of the 13,000-member First Baptist Church of Atlanta, he often preached about the sanctity of marriage and the evils of putting asunder what God hath created.

Like most fundamentalist churches in the South, First Baptist had an unwritten rule. Divorced men could not serve as pastors or deacons. That was the rule and the rule was not to be broken.

But this was no ordinary man. Dr. Stanley was a dynamic spiritual leader in the nation's largest Protestant denomination, the Southern Baptist Convention. He had served as president of the SBC. He headed his own television ministry, reached fame as a best-selling author and could mesmerize a crowd with his commanding voice.

Such a man as this could not fall from grace. If Dr. Stanley's family fell apart, how could you keep the rest of God's flock together?

"During the early 1990s, the rest of the country began to accept divorce, but there were still definite strictures against it in the South," says religious scholar James Hudnut-Beumler, dean of the School of Divinity at Vanderbilt University. "At that time, for many southerners, divorce was considered a moral failing. And if you failed morally, your church, the very people who knew you best, often shunned you. You may have been in search of healing, but all you could do was look for a different church to attend."

Charles Stanley's story is consistent with the evolving attitudes of religious people in the South and the difficulty experienced by divorcing people throughout the region. For most of the 1990s, Dr. Stanley, his wife, Anna, and the members of First Baptist followed the roller coaster path of the Stanley's marriage. As the couple battled their demons, attitudes began to change in many conservative congregations.

Fundamentalists saw the Stanleys' plight as a morality play pitting good against evil. First, Anna Stanley announced that they were separated and would soon divorce. Then they would not divorce, but would continue the separation. Church members saw the devil's handiwork in all of this and many left Atlanta's largest Baptist congregation. That included the Stanleys' own son, who formed another church.

Dr. Stanley told church members that if a divorce were finalized, he would leave his post. Some of the membership welcomed that news, while others began to struggle with the inflexibility of their own beliefs. They wondered if upholding the principle was worth the loss of the beloved minister.

On a Sunday morning in May 2000, Dr. Stanley rose to tell his stunned congregation that he and his wife were finally and irrevocably divorced. Then the church's administrative pastor told members the 67-year-old minister would continue in the post he had held for three decades. The congregation stood in unison and applauded.

The reaction of Rev. Paige Patterson, then SBC president, showed clearly the changes taking place within the religious community on this subject. He told a reporter for *The Atlanta Constitution* that he was "deeply sympathetic with the sorrow I know all of the Stanley family must feel over this. It ought to be a wakeup call for America that if something like this can happen to the Stanley family, society has lost its bearings."

Over the course of time, the idea of giving in to divorce had evolved from an individual moral failing to something akin to a disease. It was as though the infectious nature of divorce had spread to those once thought immune to it.

HISTORY OF DIVORCE IN THE SOUTH

Divorce in the South can be traced to colonial times, but few couples asked for them in those early days and few divorces were granted. The broad expanse of farms and plantations from the Carolinas to Texas was mostly rural and sparsely populated. In every jurisdiction, people divorced under only the most extreme circumstances — when a spouse abandoned the family, became mentally incapacitated or engaged in physical violence. No attorneys specialized in divorce and there were no courts that handled family cases exclusively.

Family issues were considered trivial matters of law. A woman who fought with her husband might have been described as "spirited" or "plucky." A man who hit his wife was only administering household discipline. When cases did come to court, there were no experts in divorce or the welfare of children, and few witnesses were called. It was most common for warring spouses to simply leave each other and make their way to new lands where they were not known and could make new lives. Entire communities south and west of the Mason-Dixon Line were populated by escapees from bad marriages in the northeast.

The laws governing divorce in the South are a blend of English common law and ancient Roman custom. In the early days, these laws allowed the husband to reign as a benevolent dictator. Wives and children were considered his property. Common law stripped the woman of her rights over assets brought into or accrued during the marriage, and gave the husband the right to the services of his wife. Out of this custom came the Old South tradition of the Southern Belle, that flower of womanhood that must be protected, restricted and cared for at all costs. She had little legal standing. Only through cunning and persuasion could the woman get her way.

Two wars have shaped southern attitudes about divorce. The idea of people as property began to change after the Civil War. Even though relatively few divorces were granted in those days, the whole idea of divorce frightened people in the South.

South Carolina went so far as to abolish divorce entirely between 1879 and 1948, but that didn't keep families together. Couples who couldn't get along split up without divorcing and then took up other relationships without being married. In a triumph of denial over sound public policy, South Carolina had to legislate how much wealth a married man could exclude from his wife and leave to his mistress.

The Second World War brought an even more profound rupture in the paradigm of man-woman relationships in the South. Suddenly men were thousands of miles from home. Wives worked in the factories producing war materials or tilled the fields their men once worked. Women had the freedom to care for themselves and their children the best way they knew how.

Southern women welcomed their men home at the war's end, but they didn't welcome the end of their freedom. War had disturbed the natural order of things. The Southern Belle was now an assembly line worker, so how could she return to letting her husband make all the decisions? It made perfect sense that the number of divorces would grow from the 1940s through the 60s. Splitting up became easier with the adoption of no-fault statutes in many southern states in the 1970s.

This was the Age of Divorce, from the late 1960s through the 80s, when as many as 65% of all marriages ended in divorce in the South, as they did elsewhere in the country. In the past two decades, the divorce rate has flattened to about 43% nationwide. That may seem like good news, but it doesn't signal some great societal awakening to the evil of divorce. Studies show that many people who would normally marry (and then divorce) are simply living together without the need for all the formalities. Even though the total number of divorces has receded, today there's a palpable sense of panic about divorce all across the South.

HERE, DIVORCE IS KING

Increasingly, we are a nation divided by our propensity to divorce. Sociologists and demographers have nicknamed the area of the highest dissolution rates "the divorce belt." To distinguish this area from the rest of the country, draw a line across the midsection of the continental United States from the North Carolina coast westward along the northern borders of Tennessee, Arkansas and Oklahoma, then on through the Southwestern deserts to Central California and the Pacific.

The 10 states with the lowest divorce rates in the nation lie north of this imaginary line, along with more than 60% of the total U.S. population.

South of the line are the emerging Sunbelt states, recognized for high growth, dynamic change and … divorce. The Bible Belt is the eastern portion of that area, from the Carolinas west to Oklahoma, from Florida north to Kentucky. This area is called the Bible Belt because here people profess membership in churches and other religious institutions in far greater numbers than in any other part of the country. Twenty-nine percent of the nation's population resides here, but they account for 35% of all divorces. In 1998, four Bible Belt states registered in the top five for divorce rate: Tennessee (6.4 per 1,000 people), Arkansas, Alabama and Oklahoma (6.0). The only state with a higher rate was Nevada, home of the quickie marriage and divorce. The South as a whole was well above the national average.

Herein lies the irony. The conservative South, home of moral outrage, family values and righteous indignation, is steeped in the one behavior universally condemned as harmful to those values. So what is it about the South that makes it such a haven for divorce? Many demographers, sociologists and religious scholars believe it begins with our own brand of religious zeal.

Pursuit of the Perfect Marriage

In the South, we believe God wants us to be married, no matter how young, poor or ill prepared we may be. That's the opinion of religious scholar James Hudnut-Beumler.

"As a region, we really believe in the sanctity of marriage more than people from other parts of the country," says the Vanderbilt University dean. "We live with a cultural imperative that makes it easier to form marriages. What we are looking for is true love. Finding true love is meant by God to be the right thing for all people, no matter what our life circumstances. We go into marriage believing that with God's help, we can make the most difficult marriage work."

This ideal of perfect marriage is complicated by influences that affect people everywhere, including television and movie portrayals of young people in love, the desire for material wealth and the hormonal drive for sex. In the South, though, premarital sex takes on a more ominous meaning than just raging hormones. It is the very definition of sin. Just because this behavior is sinful doesn't mean our children avoid sexual activity at an early age. On the contrary, studies show that premarital sex flourishes in the South. It's just that there is a much higher price to pay for these relations in most southern communities than in other parts of the country. To cure the sin that accompanies premarital sex, many unprepared couples go ahead and get married.

"When that marriage doesn't work," explains Hudnut-Beumler, "we don't conclude that the marriage was wrong. How could an institution sanctioned by God be wrong? We decide that we tried to make marriage work with the wrong person. And so we do it over again, and those second marriages fail, also."

The Bible itself says many differing things on the subject of divorce. The Old Testament prophet Malachi reports that God "hates divorce," while Deuteronomy 24:1 gives a view of divorce that few modern women would embrace:

> "If a man marries a woman and then it happens that he no longer likes her because he has found something wrong with her, he may give her divorce papers, put them in her hand and send her off."

At one point in the New Testament, Jesus condemns the granting of divorce "for any reason except sexual immorality." At another, he skirts the issue, refusing to say when divorce is wrong, but instead reminding his listeners about when marriage is right.

As part of a sermon titled *Jesus on Divorce*, Dr. Daniel W. Massie of First Presbyterian Church in Charleston, South Carolina said marriages are in trouble because many of us never comprehend their purpose.

Most studies conclude that weekly churchgoers are less likely to divorce than people who claim no religion and those who attend religious services less than once a week, but there are exceptions.

"Interestingly enough," Dr. Massie told his parishioners, "I have read recent statistics saying that the marriage rate among born-again believers is even higher than the divorce rate in the general populace. So current day disciples have nothing about which they can be self-righteous."

The well-publicized 2001 survey by the Barna Research Group showed that born-again Christians in the most conservative congregations divorce more often than non-Christians. Other studies lump Baptists among the most-divorced Americans.

Wick Allison, publisher of *D* Magazine, the city magazine of Dallas, chastised Christians for undermining marriage in a recent column to his readers:

> *"Conservative Christians are more likely to get divorced than any other faith group. Baptists get divorced at a higher rate even than atheists. Conservative Dallas has more divorced women than New York, Chicago and Los Angeles – those well-known dens of iniquity."*

The Catholic Church, on the other hand, doesn't sanction divorce. Their members tend to live in the North and divorce much less.

AN IDEAL BREEDING GROUND FOR DIVORCE

But the effects of fundamentalist religion cannot fully explain the divorce rate in the New South. In their seminal examination of "the social health of marriage in America" titled *The State of Our Unions,* sociologists Barbara Dafoe Whitehead and David Popenoe of The National Marriage Project at Rutgers University suggested social researchers are not really certain why southerners uncouple in such great numbers.

But a survey of social scientists and religious scholars comparing southerners to marriage-age people in other parts of the country suggests the following multiple causes of high divorce rates:

- Greater religious fervor
- Lower age at the first marriage
- Less social integration
- Lower household income
- Less education

Back in 1985, sociologists Norval Glenn of the University of Texas at Austin and Beth Ann Shelton of Oberlin College tackled the subject of regional differences in divorce in an article for the *Journal of Marriage and The Family.*

The most important variable studied by Glenn and Shelton was the age of people at their first marriage. Even today, Dr. Glenn feels the age of the person getting married is the most important predictor of marital stability. "Typical age at first marriage has gone up all across the country but still is relatively low in the Bible Belt states," he says. It is not unusual for young men in the South, still in their teens, to have families. And southern women gain the moniker, "old maid," if they are not raising a family by their early twenties.

Glenn and Shelton pointed to a decreasing amount of social integration in the South caused by rapid population growth and the movement of young couples away from their support networks of friends and family and into the large urban centers. Migratory patterns in the

New South have been from the Northeast to the warmer climate of the divorce belt. They've also taken place from the small towns to the large ones. This migration provides the region with many advantages. Businesses moving south provide ample job opportunities, for instance. But increasing urbanization also has its downside. There is less family togetherness than in small towns. The bonds to community are lessened. Urbanization has brought the New South many negative attributes, and divorce is one of them.

Money problems also seem to encourage divorce. The number one cause of argument among married couples all across this country is money, or the lack of it. It stands to reason that when you have less money, you argue more about how you allocate what you have.

All across the country, 11.9% of households live under the poverty line. Each of the Bible Belt states is poorer than the national average, led by Louisiana at 18.6%. The growth of business opportunity in the New South over the past two decades has made some people wealthy, but many of those business successes are based on the availability of cheap labor.

"Divorce causes poverty and poverty causes divorce," says Steve Nock, demographer and professor of sociology at the University of Virginia. But Dr. Nock believes other factors, while not overwhelming, contribute to a heightened divorce rate.

An example he gives is the low level of education in virtually all of these states. Divorce is not exclusively the province of the less well educated, but it does flourish in this population group. Eighty-four percent of all American adults have a high school diploma and 26% have at least a bachelor's degree. Residents of all the Bible Belt states have less education than that. None of these variables by themselves cause the relatively high incidence of divorce in the South. But taken together, they make the region an ideal breeding ground for marital dissolution.

"Because of these demographic patterns," says Dr. Nock, "there is less to keep people together when the love fades. And the love will fade, or at least lose its glitz and glitter, in practically every relationship."

A Typical Southern Divorce

In a region with so much divorce, there is no typical divorced person. Divorce affects people of all socio-economic backgrounds. Poor, religious people are not the only southerners who divorce. Extremely wealthy people with Ivy League educations and secular upbringing also divorce. But using the variables uncovered by social science, we can draw a portrait of a southern couple on their way to the courthouse.

Max and Donna grew up in a small Arkansas town where both families made a living on small farms. These are God-fearing households where grace is said at each meal and church attended each Sunday and Wednesday night. The two teenagers went "steady" from their sophomore year in high school, spending much of their time with the youth group at their local nondenominational Bible church.

Neither Max nor Donna were particularly good at school. With little else to do in their small town, they spent countless hours in the back seat of Max's 1989 Camaro, purchased from working road construction in the summer and throwing a paper route during the school year. They were in love, and heavy petting was their favorite recreation. Their pastor told all the teenagers what a sin that was, but everyone was doing it. And besides, they were careful not to get caught or pregnant.

Max was Donna's life. After her junior year, she quit school to work and save money for when they could be together all the time. Max may not have done well in academic subjects, but he was a natural at mechanics, the best shop student in school. He was able to keep his car running and train for his future.

Donna was in the audience when Max received his high school diploma. They agreed that she would stay behind when he went to vocational school in Little Rock, but that didn't last long. They missed each other too much. Just before Christmas, they got married and moved back to the city. Max was 19 and Donna was 18. They lived in a small garage apartment in an older section of town while he worked to complete his mechanic's certificate.

She looked for work in retail, but the search was futile. With only one car between them, it was tough for her to get around. If they had lived in an apartment complex, she might have found other young married women for companionship. She babysat the children of the family in the "big house" in front of their apartment, but most of the time she stayed at home and watched television.

With little money to go out and only each other to occupy their time, soon Max and Donna discovered they were going to have a baby. It was a frightening thought. Here they were, a hundred miles from home, with few friends and little other support. But when their little girl came, it was the most wonderful moment of their young lives.

Max was out of school, working as an apprentice mechanic at an auto dealership. It was one of those places spotless enough to eat off the floor. The cars were expensive, most of the clientele well off and the service staff just one big family. Max began the habit of going for a beer with the other mechanics once or twice a week after closing time.

Donna didn't begrudge Max the relaxation, although she was pretty tired from staying home and taking care of the baby all day. She would appreciate his help when he wasn't working. What worried her most was his habit of buying a round of drinks for the boys. Before the baby came, they moved into a larger apartment and began to furnish it. Max bought a stereo home theater and got cable television and a cellular telephone. They still had bills to pay from the birth of their daughter. Donna needed transportation, so they bought an old car and Max fixed it up. The money situation was tight and getting tighter.

Max and Donna began to argue. There was the money problem and his nights out. He complained that she didn't have any interests other than the baby and didn't make any new friends. Most of the other mechanics at work were divorced or had never been married, and he envied their freedom. Attractive young women who worked at the dealership or brought their cars there found excuses to speak with him.

The couple considered counseling. Because of their money situation, a private therapist was out of the question. Donna began to inquire at a couple of churches in their area, but the times for counseling were not convenient. Their problems went unaided, although they felt it was their duty to their child to start going to church again.

Still, Max and Donna grew farther apart. Her life centered on their daughter and a part-time job she took in a department store. He was promoted to master mechanic and celebrated by meeting for drinks with the boys (and girls) almost every evening. Occasionally, he would stay out all night.

After four-and-one-half years of marriage, Donna came to the conclusion that it was not going to work out. She took their daughter and moved back with her parents in that small town. Max stayed in their apartment in Little Rock. They tried living together a couple more times, but it didn't work. Then they remained apart until Donna saved enough money to file for divorce. It was final last year.

EASY MARRIAGE, EVEN EASIER DIVORCE

For every high-dollar celebrity divorce in the South, there are thousands like the one described above. That's why there is such a panic about divorce in the Bible Belt, because such divorces tear at the very fabric of society, alienating people who should be able to stay together.

Pastors are accused of failing to look moonstruck parishioners in the eye and tell them they are too immature to marry. And the governor of Oklahoma claims it's easier for residents of his state to get out of a marriage than a Tupperware contract.

Since the vast majority of southerners attend church once a week or more, church-sponsored classes have begun to give prospective married couples guidance on how to make their relationship work. Until recently, though, many of those classes were, in the words of participants, "a joke."

One Oklahoma woman described a 20-minute pre-wedding talk that passed for counseling. "Our pastor said, 'I am really happy for you guys.' He mentioned a couple of books to read. I never cracked them."

Five years and one child later, the marriage came to an end.

No state has been more willing to confront the divorce problem than Oklahoma. The state's civic leaders, who promote family values, find no easy explanations for this problem. They pushed the issue into the public consciousness by enlisting clergymen, academics, lawyers and psychologists in a high-profile campaign to reduce the divorce rate. These measures have had some effect, as noted in Figure 1 on page 38. Since 1990, the rate of divorce has almost been halved, mostly because questionable marriages are not taking place.

Divorce critics constantly debate how to accomplish their goals. Some say we should make divorce more difficult to obtain. Others say we should concentrate on marriage, making *it* more difficult and requiring premarital counseling.

The governor of Arkansas declared a marital emergency in his state and vowed to cut the divorce rate in half by 2010. His solution was a covenant marriage law that requires counseling and a waiting period before a divorce becomes final.

Louisiana originated the covenant marriage concept. Under such a contract, counseling is required before the marriage and before a divorce can become final. To obtain a divorce, a spouse must live apart from the other spouse for up to 18 months and prove one of the following:

- Adultery
- Commission of a felony and the imprisonment of a spouse
- Abandonment for one year
- Physical, sexual or child abuse

Other states introduced legislation to abolish or modify no-fault divorce. The Oklahoma Legislature went so far as to pass measures creating a statewide network for premarital education and for training secular and religious marriage counselors.

Government at all levels is becoming increasingly desperate to preserve marriage. Each state is required to explain to the federal government what they are doing to promote marriage. This is part of a new federal program to encourage poor women to improve their lives by marrying. Statistics show that married couples experience less poverty than single people. It's thought that by encouraging welfare recipients to marry, they will stay off welfare. Critics claim this effort will just lead to more bad marriages and increase the divorce rate in the future.

Certainly, the government should encourage people to marry and stay that way, if that is possible. Churches should continue programs designed to keep people together. But history tells us that throughout the South, people will continue to divorce.

What I've learned in more than two decades as a divorce attorney is that people are individuals, and they don't behave like statistics. They make foolish decisions that alienate those they love.

Laws differ across the South, but the truths of divorce are fairly uniform throughout the region. Despite family backgrounds that may be rock solid, we live in an era of disposable relationships. Most of my clients are economically advantaged, highly educated individuals from the best-known families in the South. Over the past few decades, people from all backgrounds have become more alienated from each other. Staying married is difficult. But history also shows that crafting a successful divorce can be equally vexing.

Figure 1:
Rates of Marriage and Divorce By State
1990 and 2001

State	Marriages: Rate per 1,000 population		Divorces: Rate per 1,000 population	
	1990	2001	1990	2001
NATIONAL	**9.8**	**8.4**	**4.7**	**4.0**
Alabama	10.6	9.6	6.1	5.3
Arkansas	15.3	14.8	6.9	6.6
Florida	10.9	9.7	6.3	5.4
Georgia	10.3	6.3	5.5	3.8
Kentucky	13.5	9.1	5.8	5.5
Louisiana	9.6	8.6	NA	NA
Mississippi	9.4	6.7	5.5	5.4
North Carolina	7.8	7.8	5.1	4.5
Oklahoma	10.6	4.9	7.7	3.4
South Carolina	15.9	9.3	4.5	3.5
Tennessee	13.9	13.9	6.5	5.2
Texas	10.5	9.4	5.5	4.1
Virginia	11.4	9.0	4.4	4.3
Massachusetts	**7.9**	**6.4**	**2.8**	**2.4**

Source: U.S. National Center for Health Statistics, Vital Statistics of the United States, annual; National Vital Statistics Reports (NVSR) (formerly Monthly Vital Statistical Report).

3

Judging the Effects of So Much Divorce

M any social scientists believe the seeming reduction in the divorce rate from 1990 to 2001, shown in Figure 1, is misleading. The divorce rate may be lower than it was in the 1970s and early 1980s because there are fewer marriages these days. When less people marry, divorce statistics fluctuate wildly.

We've looked at the reasons for all this divorce. What are the practical effects of divorce on our southern culture?

Too many people see divorce as the answer to all their problems. It can be an answer to whatever difficulty you may be experiencing at that moment, but that's not always the case over the long haul.

Divorce takes a devastating toll on our families. Couples become more bitter and alienated. Their kids lose self-esteem. Many of them experience life-long problems maintaining relationships and suffer through drug and alcohol dependency, lack of education and an inability to make a living. Multiply these effects by hundreds of thousands of southerners and you have a region that's growth is severely hampered.

Social scientists are engaged in a debate on the long-term effects of divorce on children. On one side is therapist and researcher Judith Wallerstein, who chronicled her 25-year landmark study of children of divorce in her book, *The Unexpected Legacy of Divorce.* Through in-depth personal interviews, Wallerstein centered on the painful search of these "lost" children, who as adults are struggling to overcome the feeling that love and trust are doomed.

On the other side of the debate is sociologist E. Mavis Hetherington and her book, *For Better or For Worse: Divorce Reconsidered.* Hetherington surveyed nearly 1,400 families and more than 2,500 children. Her findings indicate that 75 to 80% of children of divorce show little long-term damage from their parents' divorce. She maintains that only 20 to 25% of children from divorced families suffer serious social, emotional or psychological problems. While neither study touts divorce as a good thing for children, Hetherington is far more convinced that divorce does not automatically doom kids to a wrecked life.

Hetherington's work is bolstered by the new book, *We're Still Family: What Grown Children Have to Say About Their Parents' Divorce,* from sociology professor and researcher Constance Ahrons. While certainly not pro-divorce, Ahrons doesn't believe that divorce means disaster for all children. Of the 173 now-grown children Ahrons studied, she found the following:

76% do not wish their parents were still together.

79% feel their parents are better off today.

78% feel they themselves are better off or are not affected.

But she also notes that while most eventually thrived, 20% of her sample felt "life-long emotional scars that didn't heal." That last statistic proves that no matter how well intentioned you are, it pays to be wary of that fateful decision. Because of the possible detrimental effects of divorce, I begin each interview with a prospective new client by asking if he or she has thoroughly considered how life changes with divorce. For instance, most families who can barely pay for one household using the resources of two people must deal with the financial pressure of using those incomes to run two households.

The daily responsibilities of raising children are magnified when only one parent is handling them. Those responsibilities may include thousands of lunches, carpools, sports practice sessions and doctors' appointments.

WEIGH YOUR OPTIONS

Before you commit to a divorce and hire an attorney, consider your options. Use every resource – couples or individual therapy, substance abuse counseling, the words of your pastor or the guidance of a wise friend or family member. Sometimes the wisdom of others can keep your marriage together when you think it is impossible.

It may seem counter-intuitive for a divorce lawyer to counsel people on staying married, but those of us who do this work are in the best position to see what devastation divorce can bring. As citizens of this society, it is our responsibility to warn prospective divorcing people about their actions. No family lawyer with any integrity encourages a divorce unless there are extreme circumstances such as spousal abuse, chronic gambling, child abuse or another factor destroying the family unit.

Plenty of marriages can be saved if the parties made the smallest changes. If managing money is your biggest problem, talk to a credit counselor who can referee disputes between you and your spouse. If a messy house plagues you, think about hiring a maid once a week. You may think you can't afford such extravagance, but it's cheaper than a divorce and less disruptive to your family. If you fight over your children's religious upbringing, consider a compromise that practices the charity most religions espouse.

You cannot save some marriages, though. They may involve spouses who abuse their mates and their children, verbally, physically or even sexually. Some spouses spend every dollar in the household on drugs, alcohol or extramarital partners. You may be the most patient person on the planet and not want the divorce, but your spouse may believe it's the thing to do.

BASIC TRUTHS OF A SOUTHERN DIVORCE

Divorce is a matter of state law, for the most part, and state laws differ in how they treat certain evidence and what is at the judges' discretion. You will become more familiar with the divorce laws of your state as the process moves along. But there are some basic truths common to divorce in every Bible Belt state.

Truth #1

There will be a waiting period from the time you file the divorce until it is final, and that period differs by jurisdiction.

Truth #2

Your divorce will be determined by a judge or other administrative officer in all states except Georgia and Texas, which allow juries to decide certain issues.

Truth #3

You live either in a community property or equitable division state, and those principles will govern how your assets are divided. You are not guaranteed, in either case, that assets will be divided 50-50.

Truth #4

You will either have sole custody of your children, share a form of joint custody or be a non-custodial or visiting parent.

Truth #5

In almost all cases, the spouse who does not have primary custody of the children will pay child support to the primary custodial parent after a divorce based on your state's child support guidelines.

Truth #6

If parents have been involved in their children's lives during the marriage, they should have significant access to their children after a divorce.

Truth #7

Once a divorce is filed and one party wants it, you can't stop it from happening.

Truth #8

No-fault divorces are easier and quicker to obtain than divorces resulting from at-fault or covenant marriage contracts.

I have heard divorce described by learned people as a form of temporary insanity. This is true in many cases, but certainly not all. In succeeding chapters, I will lay out the rudiments of a successful divorce for those who don't want to move haphazardly through the process in an angry stupor, but want to emerge emotionally and financially intact.

When Divorce is Inevitable

Sometimes, you cannot avoid divorce, even with counseling and all the mature reflection available to you. You may not want a divorce, but your spouse may decide to file anyway. Or through no fault of your own, you have to file for divorce yourself.

A SHORT PRIMER ON PROPERTY AND CUSTODY

When you leave even the worst marriage, your life enters a state of chaos. Friends and family members perceive you differently. Your daily schedule changes. And if you have children, your time and energy are directed in a thousand different ways.

Divorce boils down to two dramatic changes – ownership of property and access to children. Envision your life with 50% or less of what you now own. How will that change your lifestyle?

And consider what your relationship will be with your children. Will you see them every day or just on weekends and in the summer?

No divorce lawyer should make a value judgment on the romantic quality of your man-woman relationship. We are not experts in that area and should leave it to you and your therapist. But where the rubber meets the road — the more practical aspects of how your day-to-day life will be affected — we can provide valuable counsel.

You've Never Seen Such Evil

If you've been the passive partner in the marriage, filing for divorce probably will dismay your spouse. Your more active partner may react violently to this action, and that reaction may shock you.

How could the former breadwinner of your family complain about child support or threaten a child custody case? Why would your soon-to-be ex refuse to budge an inch on negotiations that could settle this case and allow your family to heal?

It's as though a relatively reasonable person stepped out of the marriage and the very face of evil stepped back in, making a mess of the divorce. This can be disquieting to people who aren't accustomed to confrontation. They must steel themselves for a battle. Human nature dictates that people settle when they realize it's in their best interest.

I've seen divorces where both parties believe they were wronged. One man refused to allow his wife to have her own clothes, since they were in "his house." It didn't matter that both parties owned the house, it was jointly in their names and they both worked to pay for it. When the other side gets this detached from reality, you must hope an attorney will explain what is reasonable.

Without a voice of reason, settlement is impossible. The wife in this case said that even she underestimated the man's stubbornness. Even though he was the one inflicting punishment on her, he was convinced she had stolen from him and treated him badly.

EMPOWERING YOURSELF

Author Katha Pollitt, writing in *TIME* magazine, suggests that most people who divorce beat themselves up needlessly when they reach a critical point after reflecting on their situations.

"All over America, unhappy spouses lie awake at night wondering if they and their kids can afford divorce – financially, socially, emotionally. Where will they live, how will they pay the bills, will the kids fall apart, will there be a custody battle, what will their families say? The very fact that so many people leave their marriage for a future with so many pitfalls proves that divorce is anything but a whim."

For most people, deciding on divorce is scary but can be strangely liberating. You've thought about the downside. You know money will be tight. Taking care of children will be more difficult. And having to see your former spouse, perhaps for decades, will not be fun. But by making the decision, you're taking your fate into your own hands and that is empowering.

KEEPING GOOD COMPANY

When most people divorce, you discover your real friends. Some people may shun you while others rant about your soon-to-be ex. A long line of co-workers, friends and family members will offer advice. But none of these people know all the secrets of your married life, and no one can advise you accurately without all the facts.

People who are divorcing come to their attorneys armed with plenty of personal advice. They walk into my office with war stories about a cousin in another part of the country and what he or she got in the divorce. In fact, my first meeting with many of these clients is spent correcting perceptions about what to expect and how life will unfold.

The time to seek help from family and friends is *before* you decide on a divorce, but many people are too embarrassed to seek advice for marital problems.

Your best friends should listen calmly and simply try to be there for you. Just remember, friends and family members are sometimes brought into court to testify, especially when the custody of children is involved. Be careful which people you choose to tell your deepest secrets, because witnesses are there to testify under oath. They can't help but tell the truth. You could hear your words repeated by one of your very closest confidants. Lean on family members and friends for emotional support, but turn to an expert for legal advice.

A successful divorce begins with clear, concise communication of the facts and how to proceed.

TELLING YOUR FAMILY

How does your family react when you give them bad news? Do they sympathize or automatically blame you? Your family history can prepare you for their reaction. Prepare yourself for skeptical looks and probing questions, so you won't be shocked or upset. Someone may infer that your spouse is the best thing that ever happened to you, and why would you leave such a wonderful catch?

Little did the person asking this question know that he snorted half the cocaine in the South before beating you and the kids. Or that he or she maxed out the credit cards and left them for you to pay.

If your family members' blessings are important to you, be ready to lay out the facts in vivid detail.

TELLING YOUR CHILDREN

Correctly telling your children may be the most important chore early in the divorce. The following are pointers on how to handle this delicate matter.

- Do it soon, before they overhear you telling someone about it on the telephone or a relative does the dirty work for you.
- Do it as a couple, if you can put aside your anger at each other.
- Don't call your spouse names or do anything to make the children hate the other person. If your ex is bad news, the children will know soon enough.
- Do your best to reassure your children that they did not cause the divorce, that their lives are not ruined and that both parents still love them.

Often, this task demands the patience of Job. A woman who worked in an executive capacity was married to a man who stayed drunk and away from the house for days at a time. She took care of their three children, and he kept company with Jack Daniels. When the husband raided their teenage daughter's college fund and gave the money to his girlfriend, that was the last straw. The wife, apparently preparing for sainthood, refused to bad-mouth the sorry character to her kids. Instead, she extracted a promise that if he would return the money, she would restrain herself. Together, they told the children about the pending divorce. She could have destroyed the man in their eyes. It was tempting. But they came out better than if she had declared war. Sometimes, a successful divorce involves hard work and sacrifice. A person as rotten as this woman's husband is certain to show his true side to the children as time goes by. Or someone else will fill them in on what a scumbag he is. There is little you can add without seeming petty and vindictive.

Don't Tell Too Many People Too Early

Talking to people about your problems can be therapeutic. Telling too many people early in the divorce process can be embarrassing.

Many divorces start amicably enough. People want to be reasonable. They are thinking about the children. But as the word filters out to friends and family members, bits of information about the other spouse make their way back to you.

A barrage of facts and opinions flies back and forth. People who don't know the truth of your marriage say awful things. And then, when you've had enough, the lid blows and a divorce that might have been settled easily becomes a desperate struggle that can go on for years and cost many thousands of dollars.

Loose lips in the early stages of divorce can also cause embarrassment because couples often reconcile. There's nothing more embarrassing than criticizing your spouse to someone you know well, then having to take it all back if you call off the divorce. When in doubt, keep your anger to yourself for the time being.

Anyone getting a divorce should sit down and make a list of friends and family members to tell or who will find out through intermediaries. Decide upfront how much to tell each person.

5

Do You Need A Family Lawyer?

A cross much of the South, people are handling their own divorces in increasing numbers. Some feel they don't have the money to hire an attorney. But the amazing growth of this trend is mostly among people who simply dislike lawyers or don't trust them to pay close attention and do a good job.

PRO SE LAWYERING

Do-it-yourselfers often realize they don't understand the judicial process. But they believe their honest handling of divorce in a timely and rational manner makes up for their lack of knowledge. To their way of thinking, they could not be more incompetent than some divorce attorneys they feel are only out to steal their money. How could things turn out worse than many divorce horror stories?

Fundamental to our legal system is the right to represent yourself pro se, which in Latin means "on your own behalf." Sixty to 90% of the divorce, child custody and abuse cases in many cities include at least one party without a lawyer. In some places, that represents a doubling of pro se representation in the last decade. Judges and other court personnel refer to this phenomenon as the Home Depot approach to family court. Self-service divorce lawyering can cause logjams at the courthouse and leave many litigants unsatisfied with the results.

"They don't know how to get the forms," says one South Florida judge. "They don't know how to fill them out or what to do with them when they are filled out. Some pro se litigants drag out hearings to punish their spouses. They don't know how to ask questions or present evidence. In fact, many don't know they need evidence. Instead, they rely on their scribbled notes or accusations without backup."

In 1999, 71% of those who divorced in Orange County, Florida did so without representation by an attorney. That's up 22% from the previous year. The numbers are not as great in other southern cities, even though the courts have made self-representation easier by providing instruction to litigants.

Fulton County, Georgia, for instance, operates the Family Law Information Center that helps about 20 clients each day. The Center sells packets of forms and instructions for each action you want to pursue in court. An attorney from the Atlanta Legal Aid Society is available to provide litigants with basic advice.

In uncontested divorces, people can use these services to walk themselves through court. In more complicated divorces, ones with children, larger amounts of property or a spouse who cannot be located, litigants often start out pro se, but decide to hire an attorney after they begin the process.

The Family Court Self-Help Center in West Palm Beach, Florida offers similar services. According to court records, at least half of the 2,423 family court cases open at this writing have one or both parties representing themselves. Before the Center opened in 1996, people often turned in handwritten divorce filings and were confused about the system.

"They clogged the court dockets and slowed the process to a crawl," says Janen Moyer, a Certified Divorce Planner in Deerfield Beach, Florida. "Even when pro se litigants would win, they weren't sure what they had won or how to secure assets. Say the court awarded them the money in a bank account. They didn't know how to actually get possession of that account. They had to rely on judges to instruct them, and teaching litigants how to succeed is not a judges' job."

NO TIME TO TRUST BLINDLY

A major problem with pro se representation is that because litigants lack the knowledge and experience of an attorney, you are forced to trust the judgment of others — judges, legal aid lawyers and other court personnel — who don't know you or your situation.

Trusting in others is a virtue at most times of your life. But depending on the facts of your case, trust at this time may not lead to a successful divorce.

In almost every divorce, there is an active partner and a passive one. Sometimes, the active partner insists the couple hire one lawyer to work on behalf of both parties and simply paper the agreements they make between themselves.

A good example is that of a young wife and mother in Alabama who sought a divorce from her older, more business-savvy husband. The couple agreed the woman would have custody of their daughter. The man said he didn't want responsibility for the child, but there was one problem.

The woman only recently moved into an apartment, and the husband said their attorney, who also handled business affairs for his company, insisted the judge would want the papers to say that he got custody. It was only a formality, he told her, but it had to happen that way.

The woman signed the agreement the attorney drafted, genuinely believing she was going to get custody of their child despite what the papers said.

The husband said the daughter had to stay with him until the divorce was final, for appearances sake. But when the papers were filed, the woman noticed when she called her husband's house that his tone had changed. Finally, she demanded to know when her daughter was coming to live with her. He told her the judge gave him custody —"just read the papers" — and he hung up the phone.

This and many similar cases all across the South point up the problem of having one attorney handle all the details of the divorce. As a matter of law, in most jurisdictions an attorney can represent only one side in such a dispute. If you are the passive partner in this kind of arrangement, any benefit you may receive from using your spouse's attorney is purely accidental.

In our example, the woman eventually got custody of her daughter. But she paid an overwhelming financial and emotional price to go back to court and prove her husband deceived her and obtained the original divorce agreement through fraud. It was a hard lesson in misplaced trust.

SELECT YOUR ATTORNEY BASED ON FACTS, NOT HYPE

Even though pro se representation is on the rise, the vast majority of divorcing people all across the region find they are better off with their own attorney rather than representing themselves or depending on their spouse's attorney.

If you come to that decision, you must begin a quest for the attorney who can serve you best. That search usually begins by calculating the experience level you need in an attorney to handle your case.

As the attorney's level of experience increases, so does the hourly rate. Rates also depend on whether the attorney is located in a large metropolitan area or a small town. A relatively inexperienced young attorney who handles many different types of cases, from family law to criminal to real estate, in a medium-sized community, might ask the client to pay him a retainer of $750 to $1,500 for a contested divorce. From that retainer, he subtracts his time at $100 to $150 per hour, plus court costs and other expenses.

A more experienced attorney, who spends the majority of his day on divorce and child custody cases, might require a retainer of $2,500 to $5,000 and charge $150 to $300 per hour. Many state bar organizations identify these attorneys as specialists in their field. The Texas Board of Legal Specialization, for example, certifies attorneys in a number of practice areas including family law. In some other states, bar organizations consider specialization a form of attorney marketing they believe does not aid the legal consumer.

A handful of family lawyers, mostly in Texas, require a retainer of $25,000 or more to begin a case. They bill for their time at an hourly rate of $325 to $500.

On the subject of fees, I differ with many in my profession. I do not believe in large retainers, no matter what the facts of the case may be or the amount of money in my client's bank account. Lawyers who collect that much money often abuse the situation and give us all a bad name with the public. I charge everyone the same retainer ($7,500 at this writing) and consider it the most ethical practice.

The amount of money an attorney charges does not always reflect the quality of representation. If your divorce is uncontested with no children and little property to divide, you probably don't need the most expensive lawyer in town. Professional fees like those paid to an attorney should be an investment. If the return on that investment cannot possibly equal your attorney fees, you've invested badly.

But if you own a large home, several cars, a portfolio of investments, one or more retirement accounts, some large insurance policies and interest in a family business, you may be surprised to learn how much money is at stake. Paying professional fees to make sure you retain your share of the assets can be worthwhile.

How to Qualify An Attorney

Depending on the complexity of your marital situation, your divorce attorney will need some specific skills to serve you well. Some attorneys are very good at tracing assets your soon-to-be ex may have hidden. Others are expert mediators. A few are excellent at obtaining custody of children.

Whatever your need, there is an attorney who can help you. There are more than one million attorneys in the United States. More than 200,000 are licensed in the Bible Belt states alone.

Begin your search by asking people for recommendations about local attorneys. People who have been divorced may have the best information. The only attorney you know may practice in a different legal area, although most attorneys believe they can handle a divorce. You might be wise to ask the attorney you know to refer you to someone who practices mostly family law. Many local bar associations operate referral services that categorize attorneys by specialty or the practice area they operate in most of the time. Marriage counselors, accountants, financial planners, business managers and clergymen often know family lawyers with good track records.

Once you have the names of two or more family lawyers, interview each of them. Remember to ask if an attorney charges for this first interview, because that practice differs by locality and individual lawyer.

In each interview, the attorney will want to cover the basic history of the marriage and the issues of conflict involved in the divorce. Be as candid as possible, letting the attorney know your good points as well as your faults. Lawyers are under an ethical obligation not to disclose the information you provide to them, unless you consent to the disclosure. Don't worry that you will shock the attorney with your story. An experienced family lawyer has heard almost everything either eccentric or illegal. The worse your behavior has been during the marriage, the more important it is for your attorney to know the details.

In this first visit, a lawyer will try to distill the issues being contested in the case and summarize the major assets and liabilities of the divorcing parties. Help this process along beforehand by preparing a detailed list of debts and assets and a narrative of your marital history.

DISCOVERING AN ATTORNEY'S REAL QUALIFICATIONS

Cutting through ego and exaggeration is a necessary part of your search for the right divorce attorney. Domestic relations is a relatively new area of the law. Throughout the South, many of the men and women lawyers who refined this practice area in the late 1950s through 70s are still at work handling cases. In many ways, these pioneers made up family law as they went along. It was seat-of-the-pants lawyering back then, and often the most effective divorce lawyer was the one who could bully and bluff and bluster the most.

Times and circumstances have changed since those early days. An article in a southern magazine once gave the most apt description of today's effective divorce litigator:

*"The new breed family law specialist is equal parts accountant,
educator, and psychological counselor..."*

John Wood, a family lawyer from Birmingham, Alabama, believes family law is beginning to evolve into a more sophisticated practice. "Outside of a few major cities in the South, many lawyers still just come to court and see what happens. In the past, they've been successful without a great deal of preparation. But that style of practice is coming to an end," Wood says.

In many parts of the South, the urge for divorce attorneys to boast about their abilities is irresistible. I've heard divorce lawyers claim that when they are on one side of a divorce, the other side will just give up for fear of being crushed in the dirt. I've had clients assume from interviewing several attorneys that no family lawyer has ever lost a case. Most attorneys gladly trumpet their successes, and few tell you about their failures.

To wind up with the best possible attorney for your circumstances, clients at the interview stage must do the following:

- Ask questions of the attorney and demand forthright answers. Educating yourself is at least half the benefit of this process.
- Get a rundown of the types of family law cases the attorney has handled and the results.
- If you have a family business at stake, find out the attorney's experience handling complex property arrangements and the resources (accountants, business-related expert witnesses) available to provide evidence.
- Don't allow an attorney to generalize about past accomplishments. Demand specific information, such as the facts of each case, money amounts involved and the disposition of each case.

- If you anticipate a fight for custody of children, ask to speak with clients who will tell you how this attorney performed in such a suit.

- If you believe the attorney is exaggerating, ask for the names of clients you can call or just move on to the next attorney on your list.

- Most important, determine if the chemistry is there between you and the attorney. Your attorney will know every good and bad thing about you before the divorce is final. More than other legal specialists, the family lawyer must be someone who makes you feel comfortable.

Matching your attorney to your temperament is also important. Often, people begin their attorney search by trying to engage the meanest lawyer in town. But meanness without a concrete purpose breeds anger, which results in the need for retaliation.

Acts of retaliation by one side or the other drag out the case and cost money. What you really want is an attorney whose mode of operations fits the tone and tenor of the case. This is essential to a successful divorce.

Some cases demand a tough customer to match the tenaciousness of the other side. What you want this attorney to do is use attitude as a weapon to help you. He or she should never use your fees to feed an overblown ego. An attorney who can successfully maneuver the other side into a settlement of the case on your terms should be more to your liking.

At the end of the initial meeting, you and the attorney will determine if you are a match. If so, he or she will ask you to sign an agreement covering legal fees and expenses. Then your newly retained lawyer will give you some homework — a listing of additional information needed to prepare the case. The better you do your homework, the more likely you are to have a successful divorce.

KEEP FEES REASONABLE

Most matrimonial lawyers charge on an hourly basis for services provided by the attorney and staff members. Sometimes an attorney brings in other experts or professionals you are required to pay. The clock is ticking and money is being spent each time your attorney performs an action on your behalf – meeting with you, working on your case, assigning his staff to work on your case or speaking with you on the telephone.

For that reason, clients who use an attorney as a sounding board for all the "he said, she said" minutiae that is common in a divorce find themselves with a huge bill to pay.

Gossip, whining and endless talk will cost you money. A smarter move is to write down questions to ask and facts you want your attorney to know. You may believe a face-to-face meeting is necessary to adequately inform the attorney about you and your case. Many items can be covered by telephone or e-mail with the attorney or the legal assistant assigned to you.

Matrimonial law experts often return phone calls to clients late at night, from their homes, due to court schedules. Clients sometimes try to call then, too, just to vent their complaints. This is family or solitary time that's as valuable for attorneys as anyone else. As such, it can be expensive. Discuss with your attorney what he or she considers an emergency and how much that time costs.

The combativeness of the opposing party can greatly affect the cost of your divorce. I like to determine early in a case how much fight is in the other side. If your spouse wants his or her day in court when the issues are simple and should settle easily, you could be in for a lengthy and expensive battle. This type of opposition will often result in significantly higher legal bills for both sides.

RETAINERS SHOULD BE REFUNDABLE

A popular saying with family lawyers in certain parts of the country for several decades has been, "Gunfighters don't charge by the bullet." This means the only real measure of an attorney's effectiveness is results, not time spent on a case. Some family attorneys have used this type of thinking to justify large nonrefundable retainers.

Most family lawyers require a retainer to ensure that he or she is paid for the time spent and expenses incurred. Retainers throughout the South begin at $500 and can work their way up to as much as $25,000 or more for very complex cases involving large estates, complicated financial issues and/or difficult child custody disputes.

For decades, attorneys handling large divorce cases did not refund retainer money if the couple reconciled, the case settled or the client decided to hire another lawyer. Today, though, people are wiser consumers of legal services. Perhaps half the potential clients who come into our offices wind up reconciling and calling off their divorces. Often this happens right after we've taken a retainer and before we've done much to earn it. In almost any other commercial enterprise, people who simply change their minds about a purchase before a product is used or a service is rendered can get their money back. That didn't happen with divorce lawyers in the past. Today, though, most attorneys refund unused retainer money because people demand it, some state laws require it or it's simply the right thing to do.

Retainers are justified, if used correctly. The retainer may need to be replenished regularly, especially just before going to trial. A contested trial may take several days or even weeks of trial time and many weeks of preparation. An attorney's fees and expenses can be substantial in a contested matter.

If a client is unwilling to pay the lawyer in the midst of a crisis, it's unlikely payment will come once the problem is solved. And if the attorney doesn't solve the problem to the client's complete satisfaction, collecting for the time spent can be difficult. Knowing what a satisfactory outcome is for a client can be tricky. You might secure a majority of the assets for the client but be tagged a loser because you couldn't come away with some trivial household item of great sentimental value. That's why divorce lawyers get their money up front through retainers.

Many people who handle their own divorces try to call attorneys in an attempt to get free advice. This is similar to a person calling a surgeon and asking specific medical advice or how to perform an operation. Even if a doctor or attorney wanted to respond, neither can properly advise a do-it-yourselfer about these serious situations over the telephone, with any degree of effectiveness.

IF YOU'RE THE ONE WITHOUT RESOURCES

Your best move is to find the money to hire an attorney. In many cases, the passive partner or the undocumented spouse is also the cash-poor one. It is still common in many marriages for one spouse to control the purse strings, while the other party has little or no access to assets or large amounts of money.

The most common example of this situation is a stay-at-home mom whose husband pays the bills and gives her a monthly household allowance. Fewer women each year agree to such an arrangement.

If this is your situation, expect problems if you should ever divorce. You will be at the mercy of your spouse for the money to hire an attorney. If your spouse does not voluntarily hand over the money, in most states your attorney will have to ask for a temporary hearing in which a judge or court master can order the money turned over for legal fees.

If there are not enough marital assets to cover fees, you may have to negotiate a payout or arrange a bank loan secured by something of value. Advances on credit cards or loans from friends or relatives are also possibilities. Even a wealthy client may lack access to retainer money. A good attorney will work with you to help you find a way to secure sufficient funding for legal services.

ATTORNEYS RARELY BET ON THE COME

Like most businesspeople, though, attorneys do not favor payment methods that force them to wait until the case is over to get paid.

One payment alternative attorneys rarely depend on is the notion that one party will be ordered to pay the others' attorney fees at the end of a divorce. In past times, courts did order such payments in some instances. This practice is used less often as the court system has been pushed to become more gender neutral.

Contingency fee agreements, in which the attorney gets a percentage of the assets retained, are not allowed for divorce cases in most southern states. The theory is that with agreements like these, attorneys become parties to the divorce and might recommend courses of action that are not in the best interest of their clients.

You truly get what you pay for in life. If you hire a legal professional, you are best served by paying for professional services in a timely manner. A lawyer who goes unpaid for a long time might give you work that is less than stellar. Be clear at the outset that you are paying for only the finest professional services, no matter the fee arrangement.

INSIST ON ITEMIZED BILLS

Your attorney should provide you with regular billing statements showing the time invested in your case, the expenses incurred and the balance of any retainer. Bills should be tallied at least once a month.

Preparing a case for trial may require the lawyer and staff to work many hours examining countless documents and preparing witnesses for trial. Since your attorney has no control over the court's docket, he or she may not be able to determine if your case will go to trial at a particular time. Because of this fact, your attorney may come to court fully prepared for trial, only to have to return in a few weeks after preparing all over again.

Sometimes, clients say they want their lawyer to do whatever it takes. That is the same as saying, "I don't care how much it costs." How often in your life have you told someone that (not often), and how badly was your generosity abused? (very badly).

An instruction like that can cost you an incredible amount of money. The type of client who gives his attorney carte blanche rarely considers the range of services the lawyer might provide and add to the bill. Monthly statements that detail the services rendered are the best protection from abuse of your wallet.

Effective management of the billing procedure is another part of reaching a successful divorce.

WHO PAYS EXPENSES?

Most attorneys bill you separately for expenses incurred in a case, including filing fees, deposition costs and the cost of expert witnesses.

The average filing fee for a divorce action anywhere in the South, less than $100, is a minor portion of the total expenses. Depositions of the opposing party and some important witnesses are essential to the discovery process, which precedes a trial. Costs usually are based on the length of the deposition. A court reporter records the testimony. This service can cost several hundred dollars. You also pay for the attorney's time associated with preparing for and taking the deposition.

Expert witnesses are necessary in many complex cases. If you have a family business, an accountant or business consultant may help determine the value of the enterprise. In a contested custody trial, psychologists and psychiatrists are asked to recommend what they believe is in the best interest of the child.

Fees must be charged for serving the opposing party with pleadings, subpoenas and other related documents. A special process server can serve documents immediately, while the local sheriff's department sometimes takes several weeks. The fee for service of documents by a process server generally runs from $50 to $100 or more, depending on how difficult it is to locate and serve the individual. Many law firms charge for copies and faxes as well as other costs associated with preparing the case.

Always familiarize yourself with the anticipated costs to avoid confusion. A qualified attorney will have no trouble explaining costs to you.

FORM A PARTNERSHIP WITH YOUR ATTORNEY

In the best cases, you and your attorney form a short-term partnership devoted to mutual success. Find out what your attorney plans to do next, when you can expect the divorce to be filed and when your spouse will be served with papers. Insist that your attorney inform you about developments in the case, should your spouse retaliate in response to the divorce action and the service of papers. Your attorney should be able to advise you in every instance. If he or she has trouble doing that, a communications problem may become evident between the two of you that could become detrimental to a successful outcome.

Expect your attorney to be specific about the procedures, time deadlines and costs involved in the process. You are the boss. Your attorney works for you, and the two of you must work together.

Your attorney will give you homework that helps him or her learn everything possible about the marriage, the reasons for the divorce and the overall history of the relationship. A narrative of your married life can be extremely helpful to the lawyer and the staff in preparing your case. Be as thorough as you possibly can, to help your attorney understand what happened in your marriage. Be careful to stash this information in a safe place where your spouse cannot find it. A detailed history of an ongoing adulterous relationship or a patently illegal activity is not something you want to share with your soon-to-be ex.

In addition, your lawyer will need a list of assets and debts in as much detail as you can provide. If custody is an issue, supply extensive information about your children, and provide a parenting history of you and your spouse.

All of this is essential background information clients give me as written assignments. I need a time line of events, along with a witness list. This provides more than just the information I need to formulate my case. It immerses clients in their cases and makes them think about events that have a major impact on their lives.

Preparing Your Strategy Plan

Southerners of the old school had a unique ability to hold a grudge. You see it in the works of our best playwrights and novelists. You see it in real life, also. There is nothing more tenacious than an entire culture based on the call, "the South will rise again."

Southerners are loaded with forgiveness, but they never forget. And when the natural passion of the southern couple is amplified by divorce, you'd better get out of the way.

Northerners like to turn our passions against us for their own amusement. *Cosmopolitan* magazine talked about southern divorce in a 1995 article that proclaimed:

> "*… the only spectacle grander and more imaginative than the Southern wedding is the Southern divorce. When sweet romance suddenly goes sour, the Southern couple hits the abort-marriage button, and the fur starts to fly.*
>
> " *'I'm fixing to file on your ass!' is the war cry of the unhappy*

Southern bride. The actual filing of motions doesn't make for juicy Divorce Court drama nearly so much as the stuff that precedes the first call to the lawyer. Dixie-bred humorist Bo Whaley once wrote that he was all for women's liberation. He'd liberated one himself in court.

"Breakups can be confusing for the Southern man. He picks up an outright violent message with crystal clarity, no problem. But he's perpetually baffled by the passive assault of the wronged Southern belle. A belle will never, ever slap a man. Instead, she makes him punch drunk with praise and then takes his most beloved bird dog to the pound. Or she serves his favorite dinner, then goes outside and smashes his antique Thunderbird to dust with a sledgehammer while he's eating. Or she makes mad, passionate love to him, then steps into the bathroom to freshen up and is never seen or heard from again."

Must Hurt and Anger Rise Again?

In the New South, not every divorce has to be a fight to the death. I say this as a person who advocates vigorously for my clients each day but never lets my zealousness get in the way of their best interest.

If you want to control the conflict, keep the tone and tenor of the debate on a high level. In fact, you control the situation best when you shut off debate entirely. Many agreements that are perfectly fair to both parties wind up back in play after one spouse says something awful to the other before the final papers are executed. Or one spouse says something to a third party, who throws it back at the other spouse. Or one spouse compares settlement offers with friends and is convinced the deal is not good enough. There are many valid reasons to nullify agreements, but pride, ego and jealousy are not among them.

Decide early in the process to pursue a successful divorce. Understand that keeping to your plan will take resolve. Let your attorney know your wishes.

DOCUMENTS TO FILE

In every jurisdiction, litigants must follow certain procedures and file the correct documents. Even with an uncontested divorce, the judge needs to know that the parties have reached agreement and understand the substance of that agreement. The party filing for divorce is the petitioner and the opposing party is the respondent. If a divorce becomes contested at any point, many other documents may be necessary. The basic documents differ for each state, but they fall into the following categories:

Divorce Petition – "Filing for divorce" is submitting a divorce petition to the court. This document contains certain factual information about the parties, as well as the grounds for divorce. All southern states allow no-fault divorce, although in South Carolina you must wait a full year after the marriage before you can divorce for any reason. The catch-all reason for no-fault divorce is incompatibility, which means you have grown apart and don't believe the condition is reversible. Arkansas, Louisiana and Oklahoma have covenant marriage, which offers an at-fault type of divorce. The petition is filed by the petitioner and served on the respondent.

Respondent's Answer – This document is the answer to the petitioner's pleading. Usually, the respondent must file this document within a certain time after the petition is filed.

Inventory of Assets and Liabilities – This detailed list of everything the parties own or owe includes notations about who should receive what asset and who is responsible for what debts. This list is prepared from lists of each party. It is an agreement sworn to by the parties and filed with the court.

Final Decree – This document, executed by the judge, is known by a variety of names. It grants the divorce, approves any settlement agreement or order of the court and makes it binding on the parties.

Every state in the South has a waiting period between the filing of the petition and when the divorce is final. In most cases, the waiting period is either 30 or 60 days. In states with covenant marriage statutes, the waiting period can be up to two years. It gives the parties ample time for reconciliation or to make certain they haven't moved too quickly. The waiting period allows you time to decide if divorce is for you, and state governments want to insure that you make the right decision.

YOUR SPOUSE, FRIEND OR FOE?

If you want to remain friends with your soon-to-be ex-spouse, you may reach a point when you have to decide just how much that friendship is worth in emotion or actual dollars.

This can be a dangerous point in the divorce process, because you will have to decide how much you are willing to concede to keep the other side happy. And that decision must be made while you are most vulnerable. The steady hand of an emotionally detached party who is experienced at handling divorce matters may keep you from the mistake of a lifetime.

I've dealt with many people who wanted to shed themselves of a spouse but were panicked about losing that person's friendship. In some cases, that person made all the important life decisions for both of them and the passive spouse felt lost without that help.

Here's an example of the kind of decision you don't want to make at this point. If your spouse wants to retain the family business, and that business comprises most of the asset value in the marriage, he or she may prevail upon you to sign away the business with the promise of a return in the future. It is essential to have your attorney structure an agreement that guarantees you money for your share. This can be done by requiring insurance on the spouse's life and — if the business or another marital asset of value can be tied to the debt — using that asset as collateral in case the business fails or is later sold by the spouse.

If you become hard-nosed about your rights, know that your spouse may react by threatening to contest the terms of the settlement. That is when communications break down and progress comes to a halt. To ready yourself for a contested and difficult divorce, remember that your spouse is no longer your friend, if just until the divorce is final. After all, this person is trying either to take away your children or keep assets from you that you need to pay your bills. You can afford to be accommodating *after* you leave the courthouse with most of what you wanted in the first place.

THE WORST KIND OF HURT

In 1997, Dorothy Hutelmyer of Burlington, North Carolina did what many divorcing people tell me they would like to do. If the law won't allow them to personally pistol-whip a philandering spouse in front of the courthouse, each of them would like to sue the person who stole away their mate for alienation of affection.

Mrs. Hutelmyer captured the attention of the nation that year by resorting to a seldom-used law. She sued her husband's secretary and travel companion, Lynne Cox, in what is known as a "heart-balm" case. In the passionate rhetoric of the South, the heart is considered the injured party. The balm for Mrs. Hutelmyer's suffering was a soothing $1 million verdict in her favor.

To prove such cases, the injured party must show the marriage was in great shape until the wanton intruder came along and wrecked it. Mrs. Hutelmyer's complaint claimed she enjoyed the "love, society, companionship, support, affection, right of consortium and kindly offices" of Joseph Hutelmyer until Cox "intentionally, wrongfully and unjustifiably and with malice alienated and destroyed a love and affection that previously existed…." After a seven-day trial, the jury deliberated just three hours before awarding damages to the wronged wife.

Legal experts could not remember an alienation of affection lawsuit that was remotely so successful. Such suits date back to the 18th century, when wives were viewed as property and husbands filed most of the suits against the wife's lover. Taking a man's wife was like stealing his horse. As women gained greater legal and financial independence, states began to throw out their alienation of affection statutes. Even more states followed suit after they sanctioned no-fault divorce.

At this writing, North Carolina and Mississippi are the only Bible Belt states that have any provision for such an action. But in most southern states, judges have discretion to award an injured spouse a disproportionate share of the marital assets, retaining the principle that married people are responsible for their behavior.

Legal scholars maintain that alienation of affection lawsuits merely sidetrack litigants from the more important issues inherent in divorce today. Because they are steeped in revenge and bad feeling, these lawsuits rarely lead to a successful divorce.

Those who would like to file such a suit agree that these actions turn up the heat between the parties, and in many cases that's the point. The vast majority of alienation of affection suits are filed to extract concessions from the other side. These divorcing people have decided how wide the war should be and what style of divorce they would like. To them, gaining a little more property doesn't compare with the satisfaction of revenge and embarrassment for people they believe have done them wrong.

Making Your Detailed Divorce Plan

No matter how you want your divorce to proceed, making a fist and covering it with a velvet glove is the perfect analogy for how you should seek a successful divorce. All attorneys should prepare contested divorces as if they are rocketing straight to trial. If you settle things, you are ahead of the game. If settlement efforts fail, you are prepared for the battle to come.

Sometimes, a little saber rattling will let the other side know you are serious and fully engaged in the process. You may have to take the fist out of the glove and calmly show your strength before people will sit down and be reasonable.

7

Alternative Dispute Resolution

Any case that resolves itself without going to trial can lead to a successful divorce. In fact, mediation is the single most significant change in family law in the past quarter century. Of about 2,240 family courts in the country, as many as 20% of them offer or require mediation in child custody disputes.

The South is far behind the rest of the country when it comes to the use of mediation. Chalk it up to combativeness or a populist streak, but many southerners feel the system is fair only when we get our day in court. Besides, divorce mediation began in California, and the majority of southerners are reluctant to embrace anything that comes from the Left Coast.

But mediation is a welcome addition to the New South. Most often, it is used in the major cities. This change from litigation to mediation has been prompted by the overcrowding of court dockets and a rising concern that making divorce an adversarial process is not in the best interest of children.

In Atlanta, for instance, couples must engage in mediation before their cases can be scheduled for trial. In the outlying areas and smaller towns of the Bible Belt, mediation is often available but voluntary.

EXPLAINING THE MEDIATION PROCESS

Moving divorce away from the courthouse and into the mediator's office can often reduce the adversarial tension inherent in the process. The job of a divorce lawyer in court is to win for the client. The job of a mediator is to negotiate the best deal possible for the client by crafting an agreement that will hold up over time.

In the interest of full disclosure, let me say that I do not function as a divorce mediator. I am an advocate, solely, for my client. I've always thought the role gets confused when you advocate some cases and mediate others. But working as an advocate, I am able to settle most of my cases before they go to trial.

But I believe mediation can be helpful in cases involving simple fact situations and limited assets. The most productive mediations are those presided over by a domestic relations attorney. The basic philosophy of divorce mediation is that even two people who despise each other can reach an accord if a neutral third party, someone trained in the intricacies of negotiation, guides them through it. A divorce mediator — usually a lawyer, therapist or financial advisor — asks incisive questions, cuts through anger and hurt and facilitates rational decision making that can lead to a successful divorce.

Some mediators believe placing two people in proximity is the best way to forge an agreement. With this uncomfortable arrangement, people are more likely to agree on something and not get stuck on trivial matters.

In most cases, the actual mediation process begins with the parties and their representatives — attorneys, accountants, financial planners, therapists, ministers, friends or family — meeting for a few minutes in the same room. Here, the mediator lays out the ground rules. Then the parties are separated and the mediator shuttles from room to room highlighting points of agreement and helping the parties think of creative ways to resolve the case.

Most mediation sessions last only an hour or two at a time, but the parties can agree to stay in session an entire day or until settlement is reached. The best mediators convince people to use the time to reach common goals that will hold up over the long term.

THE BENEFITS ARE SIGNIFICANT

The following are benefits of mediation:

- Quicker and less expensive than litigation
- Reduces animosity
- Reduces caseload
- Helps with child custody and visitation

A middle-class couple who decides to do battle can rack up legal expenses in the six-figure range and take an entire presidential administration to finalize their divorce. Mediation can short-circuit that schedule at a much lower cost. If children are involved, the process usually takes six to 12 weeks. With no children, you can reach a settlement in three or four weekly sessions. Mediators usually charge less than divorce attorneys preparing for litigation.

An even more important benefit of mediation is lowering the level of hostility inherent in divorce. Even when mediation fails to resolve all the differences between parties, just the act of dealing with each other in a controlled environment and reaching agreement on some issues can reduce animosity.

Mediation has also helped to decrease the backlog of cases on court dockets in the South. In Atlanta, for instance, mediation has settled more than 70% of cases. Those statistics are consistent with results throughout the region and the nation. One mediation practice on the West Coast reports that for divorces mediated over an 11-year period, 92% were settled and didn't go to court. Of those mediated settlements, 89% remain in force.

Children benefit the most from mediation. Even though husbands and wives are parting, they still need to communicate and cooperate as moms and dads. "In the adversarial system, anything goes," says one long-time mediator. "But mediation is conducted to preserve the parental relationship, not destroy it."

BEWARE OF MEDIATION ABUSE

Critics of the mediation process often ask pointed questions that highlight weaknesses in this system. For instance, how do you reach a fair settlement when one side is hiding assets? How do you trust a spouse who has been carrying on a string of extramarital affairs? And most egregious of all, how do you mediate with a spouse who is physically or sexually abusive to you or your kids? Can you establish any ground for negotiation under such horrid conditions.

Mediation under these difficult circumstances can be close to impossible. A party hiding something or otherwise negotiating in bad faith can abuse the process. The theory behind mediation is a sound one. But like many good things that come into use on a large scale, mediation sometimes allows those who do not participate in good faith to manipulate others.

Having your attorney on hand should protect you from these abuses. In many cases, wary clients make certain the other side is not hiding assets or doing something that will harm you in the future. If you have to hire an attorney and other advisors, such as accountants, financial planners and therapists, mediation can wind up costing almost as much as going to court.

When a party does not have all this advice, a mediator will sometimes pressure him or her to accept a lopsided settlement just to get through with it. Women's rights groups have questioned the value of mediation for this reason.

Claiming that women are more often passive partners, they believe women succumb to the pressure of making an agreement because that's what they are here to do. When mediators force the parties into a bad agreement just to get it done, this does not serve to create a successful divorce. Sometimes, you must reject a questionable agreement to make the divorce work.

EVEN WHEN MOTIVES ARE NOT PURE, IT CAN WORK

Even with all the potential problems associated with mediation, I've seen clients go into the process skeptical of the other side's motives and still come out with a worthwhile settlement.

Truth and justice, as it applies to divorce, may be a matter of degrees rather than a black and white certainty. In other types of civil litigation, the adversarial system may work perfectly. But only in divorce mediation do the warring parties often have children together.

Mediation allows you and your spouse to reach an acceptable compromise between differing views of truth and justice. And it may be the most effective pathway to a successful divorce.

COLLABORATIVE LAW:
DISPUTE RESOLUTION TO THE MAX

The newest and least-tried form of alternative dispute resolution is called collaborative law, a form of "super-mediation" developed during the 1990s to ensure that divorce cases never get into a courtroom.

In its most common form, collaborative law involves the two divorcing parties and their attorneys meeting face-to-face in a series of settlement sessions that are part law and part psychology. The goal is to divorce with the least amount of left-over vitriol. Couples with children are those most interested in collaborative law, followed by those who are in business together and must continue a relationship for this reason.

What distinguishes collaborative law from mediation and litigation is the agreement the parties and their attorneys make prior to the sessions that they will settle the divorce and not resort to the courtroom. Under the rules of collaborative law, the attorneys agree that if they can't reach a settlement, they will withdraw from the case in favor of other attorneys who are then free to continue the collaborative sessions, begin mediation or go to court. This "poison pill" feature supposedly removes any incentive attorneys might have to scuttle negotiations and move the parties toward the courtroom.

In her book on collaborative law, *Divorce Without Disaster*, attorney/author Janet Brumley described how the process can benefit the participants.

"People catch on to the idea that a divorce under collaborative law can save you money. That's not always the case. But a survey in American Lawyer magazine estimates that the average attorney fees in a collaborative law case are about one-third the amount of a litigated divorce.

"Money is only one thing you save. Pursuing divorce collaboratively can save you everything – time, your children's self-esteem, friendships, privacy, assets and whatever relationship you have left with your spouse."

Although, like mediation, collaborative law is not as fully formed in the South as it is in many other parts of the country, you can locate attorneys trained in this method in most metropolitan areas. They join together in practice groups so that both sides in a divorce case can locate a collaboratively trained attorney. If you are interested in collaborative law, check out the website for the International Academy of Collaborative Professionals at www.collabgroup.com to find a practice group in your area.

"(Preparation) is the be-all of good trial work. Everything else – felicity of expression, improvisational brilliance – is a satellite around the sun. Thorough preparation is that sun."

Louis Nizer

PART TWO

Getting Ready for Trial

8

The Hunt for Information

Divorce planning works in opposition to the chaos normally associated with marital dissolution. It is analogous to the job of the wedding planner, who fusses over the details of coupling and makes sure such events are organized and worry-free. The divorce planner's work is less romantic, of course. But a cynic might say that it's more important to the continued happiness of the parties.

The Institute for Certified Divorce Planning even offers a designation to those people who want to become certified divorce planners. Most are financial planners, but they tend to get involved in even the non-financial matters affecting divorcing couples.

"Women want to know if their friends will still like them and can they keep the house," says Florida CDP Janen Moyer. "Men want to know if they are going to be able to retire. Those are questions involved with money and quality of life."

Moyer says the job of the certified divorce planner is to help the attorney by being the one to give the client instructions that will help the attorney move the case forward.

PRE- AND POSTNUPTIAL AGREEMENTS

In some rare instances, clients come to a planner or an attorney prepared to win. The most universally recognized form of preparation is the premarital agreement or "prenup." People with assets often dread the idea of marriage, fearing that a potential spouse might be more interested in a large property settlement than a long and loving marital relationship. One way to make that big financial decision and still feel protected is to execute a premarital agreement.

Originally, mostly wealthy people preferred these agreements to protect themselves from potential gold diggers and charlatans. But over the past decade, prenups have gained favor with a wider group of people whose minds are eased by the protective aspects of these agreements.

A prenup is simply a premarital financial contract to confirm or modify the characterization of property. It is common for premarital agreements to confirm that certain assets brought into the marriage by one party remain that party's separate property.

The property in question may be an interest in real or personal property, including income and earnings. This definition includes a variety of assets, including retirement benefits, stock options, leasehold interests and unsecured debt.

These agreements have become so commonplace that even people of modest means are using them. A person with a job and some liquid assets might execute a premarital agreement to protect his or her retirement accounts or future earnings in case of divorce, separation or death.

Some assets are not easily divisible, such as an interest in a family-owned business or a large tract of real estate. A premarital agreement that spells out the portion of the property owned by the spouse as his or her separate property could keep the entire asset from being divided or sold at the point of divorce.

WHAT'S PROTECTED BY A PREMARITAL AGREEMENT?

The following matters may be addressed in a premarital agreement:

- The rights and obligations to property by either party
- The right to buy, sell, use, transfer, exchange, abandon, lease, consume, expend, assign, create a security interest in, mortgage, encumber, dispose of, or otherwise manage and control property
- The disposition of property on separation, marital dissolution or death
- The modification or elimination of spousal support
- The making of a will, trust or other arrangement to carry out the provisions of the agreement
- Ownership of a life insurance policy
- Choice of law governing the agreement
- Any personal matter not in violation of public policy or criminal statutes
- Waiving of homestead rights.
- Providing income from all separate property to remain separate property, precluding creation of any community property during marriage and partitioning future earnings.

In many jurisdictions, a premarital agreement cannot adversely affect the right of a child to support in the event of divorce. Agreements for private education, college expenses or cars for children might be enforceable as long as they are found not to be a violation of public policy.

Postmarital agreements are much like prenups in the way they deal with assets, except that they are executed after the marriage. Like premarital agreements, postnups must be in writing and signed by the parties. The agreement also must show that the parties intended to actually partition and exchange property.

Through the use of a postnuptial agreement, spouses may convert community property or their separate property into the other spouse's separate property.

This partitioning is sometimes used to protect the property from creditors by putting it in the name of the other spouse. Or in the event of a divorce, the property is already divided.

How to Enforce or Break Agreements

Premarital or postmarital agreements are financial contracts that are sometimes tough to break. To contest the validity of an agreement, the party often must first show that it was not signed voluntarily or that the agreement is "unconscionable" or blatantly unfair.

If the court declares the agreement unconscionable, the contesting party usually must prove that he or she did not know the extent of the other party's property or finances or voluntarily waived such a disclosure. Breaking a prenup involves jumping several legal hurdles one after another.

In one case, an appellate court upheld an agreement even when the wife did not have an attorney, did not read or understand the agreement and had no real understanding of the effect of the agreement's terms.

One court upheld an agreement despite the husband's contention that the parties had disparate bargaining power, the agreement was signed shortly before the wedding, he did not have a lawyer and the agreement was one sided.

Another court held "the mere fact that a party made a hard bargain does not allow him relief from a freely and voluntarily assumed contract."

Because a well-written premarital agreement is difficult to overturn, don't just sign one with the idea that you will wriggle your way out of the agreement later. Both parties to a prenup should employ experienced family lawyers to review the agreements and should understand them thoroughly before signing them.

PLANNING PAYS OFF

As we said before, divorce usually is the result of a long and torturous process. People rarely consider getting a divorce one day and then actually file for it the next. Most of the divorces we've seen happen after months or years of thought and discussion.

How aggressively you plan your divorce and how intricately you prepare for your escape is one of the most controversial aspects of divorce planning. To many people, planning for a divorce behind your spouse's back for several months or a year is simply too cold-blooded. Sometimes, such planning cuts off attempts to save your marriage. If people realize what you are doing, it can alienate those around you. Somehow, acting on impulse is more widely accepted than planning carefully. But careful planning is different from taking calculated steps to hide or dispose of assets. Planning is always good, but taking steps that are unethical or even illegal can come back to haunt you at trial or severely hamper settlement negotiations.

Still, if you move into divorce with little forethought, you may be setting yourself up for a life-long disaster. Considering the dire consequences of inaction, being assertive will help you achieve a successful divorce.

PUT INFORMATION AWAY FOR SAFEKEEPING

In the South, as in the rest of the country, marriages have a certain structure determined by which party has access to what information. Most married couples include what you might call a documented spouse and an undocumented one. The documented spouse usually makes most of the money, pays the bills and keeps the records. The undocumented spouse may have lots of interests, but record keeping and bill paying are not among them. In times of emergency, locating precious records can send you into a panic. The undocumented spouse is at a distinct disadvantage in the midst of one of life's most distressing emergencies.

Take this advice to heart: Never allow yourself to be the undocumented spouse. Insist on being a full partner in the process of paying bills and maintaining records. Information can make or break a divorce case at trial. Become an information magnet in the early days of your divorce. You must secure the records so your spouse won't find devious ways to produce them at trial or make them hard for you to obtain.

The most relevant records for you to obtain are three to five years of the following:

- Personal or corporate tax returns
- Checking, savings and money market account statements
- Paid bills
- Investment and retirement account statements
- Stock and bond certificates
- Mortgage information
- Credit card account information
- Information on existing debt and other liabilities
- Long-distance telephone bills

- Medical records
- Health insurance policies
- Photo evidence of extramarital affairs, debts
- Any other evidence that establishes fault by the other side

Find a safe place to keep this information, where your soon-to-be ex cannot find it. It might be useful in court and it might not. But you want the opportunity to make that decision by having it available.

A winning case begins with having this information, but it's not a sure thing even if you have all the records. The facts of your case dictate whether you can or want to introduce this information.

But you should have information like this for reasons other than divorce. It can be essential if your spouse is very ill or dies. If you can remember, even in difficult times, to keep your family information at hand, you can exert more control over any situation and know what's at stake.

FOLLOW THE MONEY TRAIL

Bank accounts are sources of crucial information. Often they contain facts and figures known to one of the marriage partners and deliberately kept from the other. A money trail can take you into interesting places and tell vivid stories. What if your spouse claims to make $7,000 a month, but occasionally deposits $15,000 to $25,000 into his or her checking account? This may indicate large unreported commissions or bonuses. You need to know the source of that extra income, how it is being used and how you can get your hands on it, if necessary.

What if the financial figures are reversed? Say your spouse makes $20,000 a month but deposits $10,000 a month into his or her account. Where is the rest of that income going each month? The tracing of assets is a skill involving delicate investigative techniques. But reading bank statements and following the money trail indicated on the backs of cancelled checks can take you a long way to discovering why your marriage may be on the rocks.

All that extra money may be fueling an obsession to own expensive, frivolous items. Worse, it could bankroll a drug or gambling habit. It could be used to set up and operate a business your spouse wants to keep secret from you. Or it might be used to maintain an entirely new household, complete with a new spouse and children. That seems far fetched, but whatever your imagination can conjure up, we've seen people do with hidden assets.

GET THE GOODS IN HAND

Proof of wrongdoing is devastatingly effective in divorce court. Actually getting the goods on a spouse is something judges rarely see. Look at the situation from their perspective. They hear many stories about the outlandish behavior of this man or that woman. Without proof, it is so much blather that he or she simply tunes out.

Actual information obtained through investigation can become effective evidence. Long distance and cellular telephone records are great examples of evidence that can break your case wide open.

Just after your spouse tells the judge he or she does not know a certain person of the opposite sex, a known drug dealer or a gambling buddy, you introduce an enlarged phone statement with page after page of calls to that person's number. Catching the other party in a lie can affect the feeling a judge or jury has about that person throughout the case.

Many divorce lawyers will request personal and business cellular and long distance records for the past three to five years. Sometimes a spouse will try to hide those calls behind a business account. Examining that account can bring a whole new pressure to the situation. If non-business telephone calls are charged to a business, chances are that travel, hotel and restaurant expenses are charged there, also. The information could prove valuable and the guilty spouse might settle the case to keep an employer from finding out about those extracurricular activities and expenditures that violate company policy.

Catching your spouse red handed can also give you piece of mind after months or even years of suspicion. You may have wondered if you were really on to something or if you were being unfairly suspicious of the other person. Getting the information can clear up your misgivings.

Deciding how to use certain evidence is not easy. This decision must fit into the context of the overall strategy of your case. But you can't present it if you don't have it.

TECHNOLOGY AIDS PRIVATE INVESTIGATION

"Without technology, I would spend a lot more hours watching and photographing people do things they shouldn't," says private investigator Dan Herrin.

As the head of his own investigation firm, he spends about 70% of his surveillance time spying on divorcing people with something to hide in locations all over the South. A former federal investigator, Herrin has seen technology radically change the PI game over the past few years. Here are examples of the technology:

Monitor e-mail – Herrin claims 80% of the people having affairs meet their paramours at work or in certain social environments. But e-mail is their main communication medium. E-mail is becoming so commonplace in the home today that the suspected spouse can retire to a home office and spend the evening online with a lover. Certain programs available at computer stores or boutiques that sell security gear can capture e-mail and organize it on the computer's hard drive or on another computer linked to the home machine.

The offending spouse may claim it's his computer and you are invading his privacy. State and federal laws protect a person's right to privacy, so I caution you never to monitor e-mail without the advice of your attorney. The test is, does the owner of the computer have a reasonable expectation of privacy? A computer in the home usually is property of the couple, but you don't want to risk breaking the law.

"In one case like this, I worked for an attorney who suspected his wife was cheating because she spent so much time on the computer at home," Herrin says. "That was my client's computer just as much as it was his wife's, and so we installed a program that takes snapshots of whatever is on the screen at a particular time. You can archive the screen shots or view them in real time.

"We set up an e-mail account just for this and the Internet service provider directed the snapshots to us. The wife's boyfriend sent her a web cam and they were having virtual sex on the computer. A simple program like this makes surveillance a lot easier and less expensive."

GPS device – You can attach a global positioning system (GPS) device to your spouse's car that sends a signal by satellite, allowing you to pinpoint the location of the car at all times. You can't tell who your spouse has been with using this system. But utilizing a computer and a mapping program, you can follow the car's movements precisely.

Herrin once discovered a GPS device on a client's car after her husband borrowed the car and was late returning it. In most jurisdictions, your name must be on the car's title for such an installation to be legal.

"This device was about half the size of a shoebox," Herrin says. "It takes a couple of hours to install. You have to remove the dashboard —

or at least the radio — and hook it directly to the battery. This one was well hidden. It was a professional job."

Cellular telephone – One of the most effective tracking devices is a cellular telephone. It's perfectly legal to contract with a research firm to obtain a detailed record of calls to a particular cellphone. The very existence of cellphones hampers the ability of divorcing people to hide misconduct. If they fail to stop this misconduct when their attorney advises them, you can bet they won't quit talking about it on the cell. Those who think they are especially clever sometimes get a second phone and keep it in the car. But getting a record of calls to any cellphone is fairly routine.

You May Need An Investigator

The information mentioned above is best collected by a private investigator. If you try to get it yourself, you may find yourself violating local laws. And if you hire your own investigator without consulting your attorney, you may be wasting time and money. Each attorney has investigators he or she trusts and recommends. In certain cases, an investigator's work may be the most important evidence in the case. Making sure it is gathered correctly and presented to the court in the best possible manner can lead you to a successful divorce.

Even with all the high-tech tools available to aid your investigation, most domestic cases still require some actual surveillance of the suspected spouse. Dan Herrin says that while only 20 to 30% of his firm's cases involve domestic disputes, actual surveillance takes place in the vast majority of those cases.

"Much of the information we collect, such as cellphone records and e-mails, speaks for itself," says Herrin. "But most courts want to hear testimony that explains what we collected and how we got it."

It is one thing to introduce a few e-mails from an errant spouse to a lover. The other side could shrug this off as a minor lapse in judgment, proving nothing. But if you introduce a stack of e-mail messages, voluminous cellphone records, a pile of incriminating computer screen shots and proof by GPS that a spouse was in the wrong place at the wrong time, along with video and testimony about the many times that spouse was caught, this is a much more damning record and can have a significant impact on the division of assets or custody of children.

On-site video was essential in one recent case where a father sent his children for visitation with the mother in South Carolina. The video collected by a private investigator proved the woman had a live-in boyfriend who stayed at the house during the children's visitation, violating a court order. The father used this video and the investigator's testimony to affect a change in custody.

The work of private investigators can be so damaging that attorneys use this evidence to force a settlement on their own terms. One investigator in Arkansas videotaped a mother having sex in the front seat of her car with someone who was not her husband. Her son's car seat was visible beside her, although from the angle the video was shot you could not tell that her son was in it. Still, the video was so distressing that the woman settled rather than having the tape shown in court.

Not all surveillance in domestic cases is intended to catch philandering spouses. Dan Herrin says many of his cases revolve around documenting a serious substance abuse problem, a gambling addiction or criminal behavior.

"Often, substance abuse is tied to children, as far as what we try to prove," he explains. "For example, a father might drink and drive while his child rides in his car with him or a woman is caught buying drugs while her child is present. Tying the abuse to children is much more damaging in most judge's eyes."

Not all evidence gathered by investigation is compelling or necessary to the case. The report may be repetitive and simply back up evidence you already have. Still, you will have the evidence, it may be significant and you will pay the investigator for his work. Most PIs charge by the hour, and that money is payable when the work is performed. Whatever the results or however the evidence will be used (or not used), you will pay handsomely for these services and there is no guarantee the dirt dug up on your spouse will make a difference.

Hiring the most competent possible investigator is essential. As in most aspects of life as well as divorce, you get what you pay for. You want evidence that is airtight. A skilled family law specialist can discredit an investigator who is inexperienced or mishandles an assignment.

HEED THE LAWS OF SNOOPING

If you successfully record your spouse's indiscretions, you may have that party dead to rights. But before you flash your CIA decoder ring, be aware that snooping outside the law can get you in trouble.

Audio tape recordings are the first real use of technology in divorce cases, and they have been legal in some form for years. In every southern state, at least one party to a conversation must know he or she is being taped. In other words, you can tape yourself talking to another person who is unaware of the intrusion.

It is a criminal offense to wiretap or tape a conversation between two or more people who don't know you are taping them. Because it is illegal, most courts will not allow you to introduce such recordings as evidence.

Some people believe they can record calls on their home telephone as long as their name is on the account. That is not always the case. The law is not as settled, or as restrictive, when it comes to gathering e-mail messages from your home computer or gaining a record of cellphone calls.

Even discounting the legal problems inherent in modern investigative methods, getting this evidence on your spouse may not be as helpful as you think. Many judges resent what they consider invasions of privacy. However, if your spouse continually denies things you know he or she has done, the investigative tools we have outlined may be the only way to establish the truth before a judge or jury.

Follow the advice of your attorney in this matter. Only someone experienced in the family courts can anticipate how certain evidence is perceived.

Elements of A Winning Case

The facts of the incident were too embarrassing to share with anyone, including her attorney. She had been in an exclusive department store. She held her young daughter's hand. The sales clerk left the gold and diamond pin lying on a rubber mat on the counter. Somehow, some way, the pin made its way into her purse. She wasn't sure how it got there. She just knew that when she walked out into the mall, store security guards surrounded her and demanded an explanation. Her daughter began to cry and people glared at them both. She could have easily purchased the pin by writing a check or handing over a credit card. But she didn't, and it was all an unsightly mess.

The incident sounded even worse now, as her ex-husband recounted it from the witness stand. They were arguing over custody of their daughter and this incident was being used to show her erratic behavior. Once again, those in the courtroom looked at her as though she was public enemy number one. Her attorney tried to pass her behavior off as forgetfulness, but she could see the displeasure on his face.

She misunderstood his upset, of course. It was not the incident itself that bothered him. It was the fact that she never shared this story with him. As an attorney, he never had the opportunity to tell the court about this incident in his own way.

Given the opportunity, he would have brought up the incident himself, so it would not appear that she was hiding anything. He would have said it was the act of an admittedly absent-minded, but well-meaning person. She was a responsible member of the workforce — an executive in a high-tech company — and could buy this pin if she really wanted it. And she spoke with her daughter about it afterward, telling her it wasn't the right thing to do as she listened to her daughter's concerns.

Because the woman didn't tell this story to her attorney, it was as though the other side was describing a crazed thief and borderline child abuser. It was an unfortunate and unnecessary situation.

KEEP YOUR ATTORNEY INFORMED

One of the basic building blocks of a winning case is the rapport between a client and an attorney. The combination of an experienced attorney and a helpful client can be the most powerful weapon in your divorce case.

Attorneys who specialize in divorce law can often anticipate how a judge or jury will view a piece of evidence or a witness's testimony and how much information is necessary to get the point across.

Of course, digging up the dirt on the other side and sharing it with your attorney is the easy part. If you suspect something about your spouse, tell your attorney. He or she should know how to prove it and whether the information is useful. This is the value of an experienced family lawyer. Attorneys want clients who are completely truthful and whose suspicions about the other side are grounded in fact and not in flights of fancy.

Exposing the underside of your own conduct is a more sensitive matter. Understand that most attorneys do not expect you to be the very soul of virtue. You don't want to hire an attorney you are afraid to tell things that portray you as less than virtuous. You have every right to expect that your attorney can absorb the things you say and react in a productive, professional manner, no matter what you reveal. In fact, most family law specialists have heard just about everything you could say about yourself. But like the woman in our example, many of us blot out unpleasant memories. Admitting some of these things can be painful.

Your spouse already knows about your health or financial problems, your attitudes toward sex or religion and your personal habits. Some of the most innocent circumstances can lead to evidence in a trial, especially if the custody of children is at stake.

You may harbor dark secrets that make you uncomfortable. The other side may not know about these secrets, but they can discover them with a little investigation of their own. This may involve an arrest for some youthful indiscretion, a brief fling with drugs or some other walk on the wild side. Adultery is a common secret, along with addiction and obsessive behavior.

Psychologists and social researchers contend that people who live on the edge of getting caught really want to clear their consciences. Statistically, more men carry on affairs, while more women file for divorce on the basis of those affairs. If you are divorcing and having an affair, put it on hiatus until the divorce is final.

In the next chapter, we will deal more in depth with the role fault plays in divorce across the region. Let me say, simply, few extramarital relationships are worth the risk.

Even if a judge or jury doesn't punish you for your affair, simply carrying it on punishes everyone involved in the divorce. The tension of divorce is often overwhelming. Add the strain of this other relationship and you can make a huge mess. And if your marriage includes children, you are in danger of affecting their psychological well-being with such reckless actions. Remember that you are a parent first, even if you believe you are madly in love (or lust). You want your kids to remember that you thought of them first at this time of crisis.

No Settlement Without Discovery

There are said to be three sides to every divorce — his side, her side and the truth. Getting at the truth is the goal of discovery, which gives both parties the ability to obtain information from the other side concerning the relevant issues in a case.

Formal discovery procedures may include written interrogatories, requests for production of documents, requests for admission of certain facts, oral depositions and the exchange of inventories.

It may seem natural for two people who were close at one time to exchange information in a non-confrontational manner. But these procedures often become intense and highly charged debates. In the most rancorous divorces, one side may have to force the other side to produce the most basic information, such as checking account statements and tax returns. Your attorney must decide how important a piece of information is to your case and how far you will go to obtain it.

Asking and Answering Interrogatories

The first discovery tool used in a divorce usually is a set of interrogatories, written questions designed to unearth certain facts. They must be prepared and filed within a prescribed period of time. The answers are given under oath, just as if you were testifying in court.

Interrogatories may include questions relating to a party's employment and salary information, bank accounts, charge accounts, assets and debts. There may be fault questions pertaining to such activities as drug abuse, spousal abuse or adultery.

You may ask what persons have knowledge of the facts in this case. In this way, you may ascertain who might be called as witnesses in a trial or decide whom you might call for testimony favorable to you.

Since interrogatories are issued early in the process, sometimes you can catch the other side unaware of the consequences of an answer. For example, your spouse might reveal the existence of a bank account that he or she wants to keep secret. Occasionally, you can unearth an outright lie, and those lies can have an impact on your case.

If you ask questions of the other side, chances are you will be required to answer some yourself. Answer them truthfully, without giving away unnecessary information. Discuss the inquiries with your attorney to determine the best way to respond. If you answer a question incorrectly, that is not the end of the world. In most jurisdictions, you can update and supplement your answers before trial.

HANDLING DOCUMENT REQUESTS

Divorcing parties usually ask each other for certain documents needed in the preparation of a case. Often that includes three to five years of the following:

- Bank statements
- Tax returns
- Charge card statements

- Business records including contracts, commission statements
- Insurance policies
- Brokerage account statements
- Any other such evidence the party plans to use at trial

Documents you plan to submit at trial must be made available to the other side, if they ask for them. If you fail to produce a requested document, you may be prevented from using it in court. A good attorney will object to the admission of documents he or she has not been able to examine because the other side didn't produce them.

COMPLYING WITH REQUESTS FOR ADMISSIONS

Parties to a divorce often short-circuit investigations and other forms of discovery by simply asking the other party to admit or deny certain facts in the case.

For instance, your attorney may ask the opposing party to stipulate that a piece of property was owned by you before the marriage and is not part of the marital estate. Why should you make life easier for your soon-to-be ex? Part of achieving a successful divorce is cooperating on as many points as possible. And besides, the law requires that you answer the question truthfully.

If you insist that the property is part of the marital estate, you may have to expend money and effort to refute the other side's ownership claims.

You may ask the other party to admit or deny a drug addiction, the hiding of assets or something else that might be difficult to prove in court. This puts a guilty party in a delicate position. If he or she denies the allegation and you can prove it at trial, you've shown that party's capacity to give perjured testimony.

Failure to answer a request for admissions in a timely manner may cause the request to be automatically admitted by the court. So you cannot avoid answering questions without negative consequences.

DEPOSITIONS ASSERT YOUR RIGHTS

A deposition is the closest thing to testifying in court, since it is taken in person, under oath, and often the opposing party is sitting right across the table. As such, it is the most confrontational and seemingly important part of the discovery process. Depositions in divorce cases are used to learn about the other party's case or the substance of a witness's testimony.

Most depositions are taken in the offices of one of the attorneys, with a court reporter taking down everything that's said. If you are being deposed, your lawyer should be present to protect your rights. But the opposing attorney runs your deposition by asking questions about the facts of the case and the history of the marriage. This discovery tool may or may not break your case at trial, depending on how you testify and the particular facts of your case.

There are many uses of a deposition. If you are the one who filed the divorce, you must be prepared to name each and every reason you want the divorce, if you plan to use those reasons at trial. As with interrogatories, you must name every person who knows the facts of your case. Working with your attorney, you should prepare for your deposition so you do not forget critical details in the heat of the moment.

Always tell the truth in your deposition, just as you would in interrogatories and on the witness stand. Know that there are numerous strategies for telling the truth in a deposition. Your attorney should advise you about the impact of a particular deposition and the questions you will be asked.

With skill and a little luck, your attorney can use a deposition to learn the other side's entire case. In a large property case several years ago, the wife filed a vicious and accusatory pleading alleging much wrongdoing by the husband. Figuring the wife had no evidence to back up her claims, the husband's attorney insisted on taking her deposition at the very start of the case rather than after he had spent time and the client's money with other discovery. Under intense questioning, the wife admitted she had no facts to support her claims against her husband. Her attorneys simply filed the pleading as a tactic, hoping to scare the husband and put him on the defensive. The tactic backfired, of course. The wife and her attorneys were thrown for a loss and stayed there throughout the case because of a strategy gone wrong.

A deposition can be used to discredit a witness who changes his or her testimony at trial. This results in the famous courtroom question, "Were you lying then or are you lying now?" Nothing shows vindictiveness and infuriates judges and juries more than blatant lying by a witness in a divorce trial. Even when they don't catch people actually lying, attorneys use the deposition process to size up the opposing party and determine how that person will appear on the witness stand. It is important to prepare for your deposition and then make notes of what was said for use at trial.

Often a party will use the deposition to scare the opposition, giving a taste of the confrontational atmosphere to expect if the case goes all the way to trial. This tactic can be an expensive one for the party scheduling the deposition. But if it helps to forge a settlement and avoid a trial, it can save money and trouble in the long run.

Before you schedule the deposition of your estranged spouse or other witnesses, know what information you intend to get and if that information is essential to your case. And try every way possible to settle the case to avoid the expense. If you are especially curious about a bank account you suspect has a few hundred dollars in it, there are other ways to get that information. If that account could have many thousands of dollars in it, or if custody of your children is at stake, a deposition can be a worthwhile investment.

10

Fault Plays Big in the South

Mississippi Gov. Ronnie Musgrove announced last week he was divorcing after 24 years of marriage. "We have agreed to disagree on those issues, set them aside, come together with an amicable agreement to provide for two outstanding, wonderful children," the governor said at a news conference. "Both of us agree fault is not an issue."

Christian Science Monitor

THE ROLE OF FAULT IN A NO-FAULT WORLD

We live in a no-fault world, especially where divorce is concerned. Since 1969, when then-California governor Ronald Reagan signed the first no-fault divorce statute into law, southern lawmakers have followed the rest of the nation by adopting varying forms of no-fault divorce.

Before the new statutes were adopted, this is what divorce looked like: two perfectly normal married people found themselves falling out of love and with lives heading in opposite directions. There were no affairs, no addictions, and no obsessions, just two people who no longer wanted to be married to each other. But to get out of the marriage, one party had to make up awful things about the other. It was a cruel process, having to fabricate a reason to dissolve the marriage. And it often led to a lifetime of bitterness.

Because of no-fault, divorcing people don't have to play the blame game. You can get your divorce if you simply grow apart. In legal terms, it is called irreconcilable differences. But fault still does play a part in divorce proceedings across the South.

It is in this discussion of fault versus no-fault that you catch a glimpse of the evolution of the Old South into the New South. The Old South is still alive in the region's small towns and rural areas. In the less urbanized areas, especially, there is still the feeling that people must pay for their sins.

"Fault is big here," says John Witte, director of the law and religion program at Emory University School of Law in Atlanta. An expert on the ways religion and ethics influence the law, Witte says you should not be fooled by the fact that fault is not the basis for most divorces in the South. Instead, judges and juries use fault in a marriage to punish wrongdoers and attempt to ease the pain of those parties who have been wronged.

"Our judges employ fault along with the law to decide how property will be divided and to decide issues like child custody and alimony," he explains. Fault is especially used as a response to adultery, which Witte says is considered "the sin above all others. Unlike much of the country, southerners still believe in moral accountability as a noble aim if not a reality."

While the smaller towns have their own flavor, Witte says cities like

New Orleans, Atlanta and Charlotte are difficult to distinguish from Los Angeles or Chicago in terms of attitudes and cultural beliefs. The laws of most southern states give judges in both large cities and small towns wide discretion to enforce social mores.

Family court judges would rather not deal with fault in a marriage. But with the responsibility for property division and the awarding of child custody or substantial visitation, judges often get called upon to make a moral judgment of who did what to whom and, therefore, who deserves additional consideration. Under the moral code at work in the South, fault defines that consideration and makes the issue of fault more complicated than ever before.

Whether yours is a community property state or one that mandates an equitable division of property, the court will attempt to divide the marital assets and debts of the marriage in a fair and equitable manner. It is not true, as some people believe, that only in community property states does a judge have the power to divide assets. Under this misconception, the person who actually purchased an asset would keep it in a non-community property state.

If the parties cannot agree on the division of property, the judge will determine, based on the facts, what kind of division is fair and equitable. Those facts might include the length of the marriage, the ability of the parties to make a living after the divorce, the assets and debts in question and who gets the children. Who's at fault for the divorce, along with the type of fault, is often the tiebreaker.

TYPES OF FAULT

What people claim as evidence of fault for the divorce might amaze you. Sometimes these include the fact that the soon-to-be ex failed to support her family or that she refused to cook the dishes his mother used to make. Certainly these are evidence that this person did not meet your expectations, but they aren't what the court would consider fault. Examples of fault for a marital breakup are:

- Adultery
- Drug use
- Alcoholism
- Physical abuse of a spouse or child
- Mental abuse of a spouse or child
- Sexual abuse of a spouse or child
- Overly suspicious or obsessive behavior
- Gambling
- Excessive spending
- Mental illness or psychological problems
- Criminal convictions
- Unusual sexual practices
- Long absences from home

PROOF AND ACCUSATIONS NOT THE SAME

Ask yourself if your spouse shows signs of one or more behaviors on the list of faults? We're not talking about petty annoyances, but acts that disrupt the marital union.

Often people come to court with such minor complaints that it's obvious they are as much at fault for the divorce as the other party. If you can list two or three factors that prove your spouses' fault, you next have to ask yourself if you can prove them. Let's face it. People usually don't come to court wearing signs that proclaim their guilt. The transformation people can make from the real world to court can be amazing. If you've seen news footage on television of someone being taken to jail and then see that person in court, you'd be amazed that it's the same person. You can't expect your spouse to walk into the courtroom looking like he did the last time he beat the children. You won't see him dramatically admit his guilt and throw himself on the mercy of the court.

Your proof can be witnesses, you and others. It can be a paper trail of credit card receipts, bank withdrawals and check stubs. It can be photographs, video and audio recordings. But there must be proof, or you can come out looking like a vindictive spouse who's just making things up.

The courts often utilize what is called a "reasonable person's standard" based on all the evidence. The judge often considers whether the evidence indicates the behavior of a married person properly executing family duties. Most people in successful marriages are not seen in bars late at night hanging all over people of the opposite sex other than his or her spouse. They don't gamble away their mortgage payment or purchase drugs instead of groceries. Remember, your judge probably will be married and have a keen sense of what actions are reasonable in a marriage.

If you are guilty of marital misconduct, you need to consider how your actions will seem to an experienced finder of fact. In most situations, your attorney will put the burden on you to explain these circumstances. If you are not guilty, you and your lawyer must decide how to combat the misconceptions.

Whether you or your spouse is accused of an indiscretion, concrete proof must establish guilt. You can't rely on speculation and rumor, which are not admissible as evidence in court.

Figure 2:
Grounds for Divorce
And Residency Requirements

State	No Fault Only	No Fault and Traditional[1]	Incom-patability	Living Separate for...	Judicial Separation[2]	Durational Requirement[3]
Alabama		X	X	2 years	X	6 months
Arkansas		X		18 mos.	X	60 days
Florida	X					6 months
Georgia		X				6 months
Kentucky	X			60 days	X	180 days
Louisiana		X		6 mos.	X	6 months
Mississippi		X				6 months
North Carolina		X		1 year	X	6 months
Oklahoma			X		X	6 months
South Carolina		X		1 year	X	3 months
Tennessee		X		2 years	X	6 months
Texas		X		3 years		6 months
Virginia		X		1 year	X	6 months

Source: Excerpted from Chart 4: Grounds for Divorce and Residency Requirements, Family Law Quarterly, Volume 37, No. 4, Winter 2004. Copyright 2004 by the American Bar Association. Reprinted by Permission.
1. All other grounds besides no fault and incompatability, including fault grounds.
2. To file as separate and apart, must be legally separated by court order.
3. How long you must be a resident of the state before filing for divorce.

Responding to Domestic Violence

Intimate partner violence — crimes committed by a current or former spouse or boyfriend — is the number one cause of injury to women in this country. According to a study by the Federal Bureau of Justice Statistics, more than one million of these crimes were committed in 1998, and 85% were against women.

Women in the South are probably no more threatened by domestic violence than women in other parts of the country. But statistics show that in the Bible Belt states, rates of total violent crime and crimes involving firearms are well above the national average.

PREDICTING DOMESTIC VIOLENCE

The National Coalition Against Domestic Violence issues the following guidelines to predict the occurrence of violence against women. These signs usually precede actual abuse and may serve as clues to abuse to come.

Did he grow up in a violent family?

Does he tend to use force or violence to solve his problems?

Does he abuse alcohol or other drugs?

Does he have strong traditional ideas that a woman should follow her husband's wishes and orders?

Is he jealous of your other relationships, even with other women friends and family members?

Does he have access to guns, knives or other lethal weapons?

Does he become angry if you do not fulfill his wishes or if you cannot anticipate what he wants?

Does he go through extreme highs and lows, almost as though he is two different people?

When he gets angry, do you fear him?

Does he treat you roughly, physically forcing you to do what you do not want to do?

For many people, it is difficult to examine this list and admit to being part of an abusive relationship.

SIGNS OF PHYSICAL ABUSE

It may sound like a simple thing, recognizing when you are being abused. But that is not always the case, especially with people who are in denial about their domestic situation.

The most common signs of physical abuse are:

Does your spouse hit or kick you?

Are you threatened with guns or other weapons?

Do you endure screaming or threats?

Does your spouse break items in your house?

Are you forced to submit to sex?

Is your spouse insanely jealous?

Is there anger if you don't follow orders or advice?

Does your spouse threaten to harm you (or your children)
if you leave?

If any of these signs apply to your relationship, take action immediately to protect you and your children. If you feel threatened, stay with family members, friends or in a shelter until you can obtain relief in court. When you are settled, get professional help to explain the options you may have, such as filing for divorce.

ASK FOR HELP

When you feel threatened, call the police. They can intervene immediately to help you. If you face a choice of either calling the police or leaving, get to a secure place and then call. If the police have enough evidence, they can arrest your spouse on the spot. The authorities may ask you to press charges. This process usually involves you swearing to the offense before a magistrate in the jurisdiction where the abuse occurs. Once the warrant has been issued, the police will arrest your spouse and the case will be set for trial.

Women's advocates are frustrated by the fact that this is often a lengthy and involved process. If this is the first offense, the court may recommend counseling rather than jail time. The sooner you establish a history of behavior, the more likely the court is to put your spouse in jail and keep him there.

Every 15 seconds, a woman is abused in this country. If you are in a situation like this, seek help immediately, before it escalates to something fatal. The most traumatic type of case we deal with involves sexual abuse of a young child by a parent, close friend or family member. Cases like this can occur in any racial, ethnic, religious or economic group, and even in the wealthiest of families.

PROVING ABUSE IN COURT

Once you seek help, the next important step is to prove to the judge that you are suffering abuse. For you and your children, documenting abuse is essential. This can be done with sound medical evidence, including doctors' reports and photographs. A photograph of your bruised face is the most powerful evidence you can present at trial.

This visual evidence should be backed up by testimony from your family doctor or pediatrician. This person can be a great source of immediate assistance and direct you to other professional help. If child abuse is indicated, many states require your doctor to report it to state or local authorities.

Some child protective agencies may decide to take the child out of harm's way. Your actions may start a chain reaction that you cannot stop once you seek professional help. You need to make all the necessary preparations to deal with what will follow, including possibly seeking legal advice concerning a divorce.

DIVORCE EDUCATION CLASSES

Our perception of what constitutes child abuse has changed in the last two decades. What we once called corporal punishment is now considered child abuse by many in the social science community.

Arguments between parents during divorce are increasingly thought to be abuse. Children often blame themselves for the breakup. Hostility during the divorce process only bolsters those feelings, which can lead to depression and unhappiness. Because of this downward spiral, there is a trend across the country toward instruction for parents and children to lessen the rigors of divorce.

Only in the past few years has this trend taken hold in the South. The growth of such programs has been dramatic as state and county governments, as well as the courts, have begun to mandate classes. The number of counties, parishes and cities in the South offering divorce education has increased from 125 in 1994 to more than 500 in the new millenium. These classes are available in only 37% of governmental jurisdictions across the Bible Belt, but more are beginning every day.

Churches, nonprofit social service agencies and private therapeutic practices all across the region administer programs to address the need. Clients often attend weekly classes and support groups during the most difficult period of a divorce. In most cases, children meet with other children under the guidance of a trained professional counselor to discuss their feelings and the problems they face with divorce. At the same time, parents meet with other parents and get information about how these situations are affecting the kids. Customarily, the family pays a nominal fee for the classes.

Because these classes are often required before a divorce can be heard in court, most people go into such programs feeling they are an unnecessary and unwarranted intrusion in their private lives. But surveys of those who complete classes indicate a belief that they are worthwhile.

"The primary purpose of these programs is to help children adjust to divorce," says Dr. Joe Brown, director of the Families in Transition (FIT) program at the University of Louisville. "When parents are able to work cooperatively to meet the needs of their children, it decreases the likelihood that they will return to court to resolve their differences."

In the past decade, FIT has served more than 10,000 families who were required to attend the sessions by Kentucky family court judges. FIT is now expanding into Maryland and Connecticut and even offers classes in Ireland, which began to allow divorce only a few years ago.

Features of the FIT program are similar to other divorce education classes offered throughout the South.

Parents and children attend three group classes (one per week) lasting two to 2 1/2 hours each week. One parent and the children attend concurrent but separate sessions, while the other parent attends the class at a separate time. People can register for classes at a social service agency, church family life center or recreation center near where the family lives, the parents work or the children go to school.

Dr. Brown says the goals of Families in Transition, similar to goals of other divorce education programs, are to:

• Increase a child's competence by teaching specific skills to identify divorce-related feelings;
• Reduce a child's feelings of isolation and misconceptions about divorce;
• Increase a child's awareness of how divorce affects his or her parents;
• Teach a child appropriate responses to anger;
• Develop the competence of parents by teaching skills to handle a child's divorce-related concerns.

The major cities of the South have many divorce recovery programs. If you live in a small town or rural area, you might have trouble finding a program. But most judges and court-appointed social workers can guide you to one.

Bev Bradburn-Stern, who developed the Children Cope with Divorce (CCWD) program for Families First, an Atlanta-based social service agency designed to combat family violence, wrote in the program's newsletter that what hurts children is not the reality of conflict between parents, but the ways in which conflict is expressed.

"Parents, preoccupied by constant interpersonal hostility, simply cannot put sufficient energy into their parenting roles. It is the resulting disruption of parenting that most harms children, whether or not a divorce occurs. This differs significantly from the impact of periodic episodes of mild conflict."

ONE SOUTHERN TOWN'S DIVORCE EXPLOSION

May 2, 2004

An All-American Town, A Sky-High Divorce Rate
By PETER T. KILBORN

ROANOKE, Va.

Marriage might be in the spotlight as the American ideal for many people these days. But the inescapable image for Roanoke, the all-American hub of southwestern Virginia with Norfolk Southern railroad tracks slicing through the pretty brick facades of the restored downtown, is Splitsville East.

About one in 10 American adults are divorced or separated. In Roanoke, a city of 94,000 that has taken a disproportionate share of the cultural and economic blows that shatter marriages, the rate is closer to one in five. The national rate of divorce and separation grew 10 percent in the 1990's, according to the 2000 census. It grew about 30 percent in Roanoke.

Divorce so occupies this city that the big First Baptist Church downtown is organizing "pre-engagement" classes for dating teenagers. Under a new Virginia law, courts deny divorce decrees until parents take four hours of classes to learn to help their children deal with divorce. Divorcing parents can also enroll children ages 8 to 12 in the Family Service of Roanoke's eight-week course for coping with a split-up family. And domestic relations lawyers and mediation services have bloomed along Campbell Avenue, downtown Roanoke's busiest street.

The decline in marriage mirrors the jolts that Roanoke's economy has suffered over the last decade. "Things have dramatically changed since the North American Free Trade Agreement was implemented 10 years ago," said David Beidler, a lawyer at the Legal Aid Society of Roanoke Valley.

From 1993 to 2001, about 25 percent of the area's jobs in metalworking, furniture and textile plants, which paid $600 to $800 a week, folded or went abroad. The city has low unemployment, but jobs in stores and services that pay $200 to $500 a week have left some two-worker families making less than what a single worker had once earned.

One result is a median family income of $37,826, far below Virginia's median of $54,169. That has left 22 percent of families with children, many of them two-worker families, in poverty — twice the state's rate.

Far-removed events have also worked to rip apart ordinary lives. At the Rescue Mission homeless shelter here, war is an issue.

"I'd say 25 to 40 percent of the men in the shelter are veterans," said the shelter's director, Joy Sylvester-Johnson. "Many were married and aren't married now. We've had Desert Storm people and families of people in Iraq. Not everybody comes back O.K."

A divorce is harder to get in Virginia than in many other states. But in some ways, Roanoke seems more exposed than most cities to the influences that lead to marital tensions, like poverty and lost jobs and shifting cultural views that make marriage optional.

Clifford R. Weckstein, a Circuit Court judge here, says he is seeing less and less commitment among couples. "We are tending toward majority nonmarried cohabiting couples for the first time in history," he said. "My perception, both from uncontested divorces and contested divorces, is that we are at an all-time high in people not willing to devote the effort to work together to get through difficult times."

Nationwide, 11.9 percent of Americans 15 and older told the 2000 census that they were divorced or separated. In Roanoke, the rate was 17.8 percent. For counties and a few cities like Roanoke that are organized like counties, the census ranked Roanoke first in divorce and separation among those of more than 75,000 people, with no more than 3 percent in prisons or other institutions.

Ranked another way, among cities of comparable size, only Reno, the Las Vegas suburb Paradise, and Flint, Mich., ravaged by the loss of well-paid jobs in automobile plants, have higher rates. Two other cities match Roanoke: Gary, Ind., sunk by the disappearance of steel mills, and Miami Beach.

The national divorce rate has shown some signs of ebbing since the 1990's, but the marriage rate is ebbing more, leaving fewer marriages to end in divorce and raising the numbers of unwed parents who are breaking up.

And there is little evidence to suggest that the trend toward marrying later in life will lead to fewer divorces. Surveys of the National Center for State Courts in Williamsburg, Va., for 1996 through 2001 show divorce filings slipping just 1 percent, but also find a 46 percent surge in child custody cases.

Divorce filings in Circuit Court in Roanoke show that lawyers filed 539 divorce complaints last year. Over a four-week stretch this winter, 39 people, mostly women, completed filings. They included one couple who separated after two weeks of marriage and another after seven months, but on average the separations began in marriage's year of the itch, the seventh.

Adultery, still grounds for divorce in Virginia, was cited in just 3 of the 39 cases, but lawyers say it is a factor in far more broken marriages than that. "I'm not a Bible thumper," said David Weaver, a divorce lawyer who caters to affluent clients. "But if it weren't for sex, I wouldn't be in business." Clients, he said, "come here and say they 'want space.' Well, they want space for a reason."

Connie Owens's marriage toppled when her husband, a truck driver, kept leaving and then coming back. He finally left her, she said, with their trailer, her job in a factory making boxes and their 14-year-old son. "I didn't have the heart to tell him he didn't have his daddy to walk into the yard anymore," said Ms. Owens, 51. "But he begged me. He wanted to go to his dad in Florida, so I let him. I cried until I could get down there."

Ms. Owens settled nearby in a one-bedroom trailer and found a job. "I lived there five years," she said. "He lived with his dad."

Ellen Brown, a divorced 52-year-old mother of three and the director of a program to help homeless and divorcing families at Total Action Against Poverty, a nonprofit community service agency, said, "The culture sets couples up to fail."

"There's so much societal pressure, media pressure for people to have this, have that, look this way, have a partner, have a family that looks like this," Ms. Brown said. "All that contributes to the dissolution of relationships and marriage."

For most women, divorce still spells a shrunken standard of living. Courts order little if any alimony for working women these days. Women earn 70 to 80 percent as much as men in similar jobs and receive lower Social Security and pension benefits.

But women's economic gains in recent years also seem to have affected divorce rates. While men have been losing industrial jobs, women have surged into professional and management careers that provide the wherewithal to support a family or flee a soured marriage.

"Women who have already been working for pay and get divorced," said Toni Calasanti, a sociologist at Virginia Tech here, "they're not necessarily going to be thrown into 'My gosh, what am I going to do now?'"

Theresa Scott, 49, the mother of two grown daughters, said she and her husband were executives, each earning $45,000 a year, when they broke up 11 years ago.

"My divorce was friendly," Ms. Scott said. "We planned it like our wedding. We wrote our separation agreement over pizza. He signed the house over to me. He got a condo. He got a credit card. I got a credit card."

Still, she said, "I felt stifled, resentful and angry."

"I thought life had something greater for us," Ms. Scott said. "I believe the Lord said, 'Your priority is your kids.' We don't share the joy of our kids as a couple. The hardest thing in divorce is losing control of when you see your kids."

Laurie Gearheart, 41, first married at 22 and had the first of her two children at 24. "I got a college degree," she said. "I'm a C.P.A. He had not gone to college. He did odd jobs."

"He was raised in a home where his mother cooked and cleaned," she said. "'Where's my dinner?' he'd say. As soon as I would walk in the door from work, he would go, 'Here,' thrusting the baby at her.

She divorced him and met another man, who like her was an accountant. "He was cute and charming," Ms. Gearheart said. They were married. But that marriage, too, ended in divorce, three years ago.

For marriage to work, some divorced people here say, it needs a second act. Lloyd Merchant, 40, a state probation and parole officer, was 21 the first time he married, as was his wife. After 13 years and a son, she filed for divorce.

"I wish I had waited until I was in my 30's," he said. "I would have decided who I am, what I want to be."

Five years ago, he married again. "It's great," he said. "This lady, we talk about everything. We have a friendship, too. We do things together. There's no 'woman' chore, no 'man' chore. We've got a lot of stuff in common."

Copyright © 2004 by The New York Times Co. Reprinted with permission.

Marriages don't last. When I meet a guy, the first question I ask myself is: "Is this the man I want my children to spend their weekends with?"

Comedian Rita Rudner

PART THREE

Access to Children, Dividing Property

12

Fighting for Your Children

The question of where the children will live after a divorce has roughly followed changes in man-woman relationships over the decades. In the 19th century South, it was customary that all property in the marriage not specifically owned by the woman belonged to the man, and children were often considered part of that property. In some jurisdictions, there was no provision for divorce. If a marital split occurred, often the woman was simply forced off the land and left to fend for herself.

If the husband was a man of acceptable reputation, the children often stayed with him. In an agricultural economy, this was essential because the man needed help tending the fields and feeding the flocks. With few resources, the woman was unable to care for the children and she was often removed completely from their lives.

In the early 20th century, women won the right to vote along with a steady increase in the overall level of their rights. Laws recognizing divorce all across the region were written with the understanding that women needed assets to help them provide for their children. Two world wars in the first half of the century took millions of men away from their families. Women cared for their children alone.

With increases in divorce after World War II, women gained a special status in relation to children. Custody was rarely contested, and children automatically stayed with the mother unless she abandoned them or the father could prove the mother was unfit. The late 1940s through the early 1960s were a time when husbands went to work and wives stayed home. Divorcing fathers would have been considered peculiar if they went to court asking for the kids. This standard continued until the late 1970s. It became acceptable for teenagers to live with their dads, but babies and toddlers in the "tender" years were thought to be much better off at home with their mothers.

In today's New South, many women work outside the home. Their careers consume much of their energy and sometimes they spend less time at home than their husbands. The care of children is increasingly shared between the parents. With these changing social mores, men are asking for custody more often, and it is being granted by a legal system striving for gender neutrality.

A man who comes into the process prepared to care for children stands an almost equal chance of gaining custody in many jurisdictions. Judges are more amenable to installing men as primary caregivers. And more men are stepping forward, asking for custody.

The standard used in courts today has changed from an emphasis on the rights of the mother or father to what's in the best interest of the children.

TYPES OF CUSTODY

Whether the parties agree on where the children will live or the court awards custody, you will wind up with an arrangement that is either sole custody or joint custody. Your rights under the different custody arrangements can vary greatly.

Under a sole custody arrangement, one parent has the legal right to the care, custody and control of the minor children. Even under this arrangement, the other parent is rarely excluded from the children's lives. He or she receives specific visitation rights, often under standard guidelines that are part of that state's family code.

If you receive sole custody, the children live with you. Typically, you have the right and the responsibility to make most of the major decisions for the children. This includes establishing the children's primary residence and making all medical, educational, academic and social decisions when the children are with you.

The parent without custody often has significant rights to consultation on major issues and information concerning school, health and other decisions. That parent also has rights to handle important matters on an emergency basis when the children are with that parent.

Joint custody is available in some form or another in all southern states, but rarely will children spend an equal amount of time with each parent. The way joint custody is carried out can vary widely from one jurisdiction to another. In some states, one parent is designated the primary custodian and the divorce decree specifies the children's primary residence and what decisions are to be made by which parent. In others, joint custody means the sharing of certain parental rights and duties, and the method of arriving at decisions is left to the parties.

In this less-defined arrangement, there are two types of joint custody. Joint legal custody means that both parents share rights and responsibilities, in some manner, for major decisions concerning the child; joint physical custody means that the parents share physical custody in a way that insures the child will have substantially equal time and contact with both parents.

Not all southern states make fine distinctions in the types of joint custody. In those states that distinguish one from the other, such as Georgia, the court may order joint legal custody, joint physical custody, or both. It's important to note that in almost all joint custody situations, judges insist that there be an ultimate decision maker or that a mechanism be established to make decisions in the event of disagreement.

WHEN IS SOLE CUSTODY APPROPRIATE?

Although joint custody has gained favor throughout the South, there are circumstances in which sole custody is the only real option. Sole custody is often awarded when any of the following are true:

- One parent is completely absent or drops out of sight.
- One parent is unwilling to share responsibility for the children to cooperate in the making of decisions on their behalf.
- One parent is unable to participate in decision making due to some form of incapacity.
- One parent is proved to have harmed the children or the other spouse either physically, mentally or sexually.
- The enmity between parents is so great that to force them to cooperate could be injurious to the children.
- One parent is truly unfit.

WHEN THE LAW FAVORS JOINT CUSTODY

In the past decade, joint custody has become an important feature of family law in the South as well as the rest of the country. Once it was considered suitable only for divorcing parents who could settle disputes involving their children in a civilized manner. Therefore, it was ordered only when both parties asked for it. Joint custody is often an important element of a successful marriage dissolution today, because it forces parents to look beyond their own disagreements and focus on the long-term well-being of their children. In some states, courts can impose joint custody even when there is no agreement between the parents. Now parents who cannot stand the sight of each other can be forced to work out differences for the kids' sake.

One family therapist told about a Louisiana father's ritual when he brought his son for an alternating week with the mom. The father had his son strip down to his shorts in the driveway of his ex-wife's home each time. He didn't trust the mother to wash the boy's clothes or return them the following week, so he made certain to take the clothes back to his house.

This is the height of mistrust in a joint custody arrangement, but many such schemes have provisions that allow this over-the-top behavior. But even with the drawbacks, joint custody allows both parents to retain some control over their children's lives. Parents avoid the stigma of giving up custody of their children or having it taken away by the courts.

Countless studies of divorcing families with children show conclusively that while joint custody isn't the perfect solution for all situations, children raised under a co-parenting plan do better than those in sole custody.

Psychologist Robert Bauserman of the Maryland Department of Health and Mental Hygiene conducted a meta-analysis of 33 studies between 1982 and 1999 that examined 1,846 sole-custody children and 814 joint-custody children as well as kids in 251 intact families.

Bauserman found that children in joint-custody arrangements had fewer behavior and emotional problems, higher self-esteem, better family relations and school performance than children in sole-custody arrangements. Most studies show that children in joint-custody arrangements are virtually as well adjusted as those in intact families.

He didn't report on the inevitable problems between parents or among parents and children, but concluded that joint custody worked for children, "probably because joint custody provides the child with an opportunity to have ongoing contact with both parents."

JOINT CUSTODY WHEN DECISION MAKING IS PRE-DETERMINED

The following language contains the typical terms in a joint custody agreement that spell out who makes certain decisions. This language is written just as it might be in your decree of divorce. Pay particular attention to how this language might apply to everyday life:

The Court, having considered the circumstances of the parents and of the children, finds that the following orders are in the best interest of the children.

It is ordered that John Doe and Mary Doe are appointed custodians of the following children: Sarah Doe and Thomas Doe.

It is ordered that, at all times, John Doe and Mary Doe, as joint custodians, shall each have the following rights and duty:

1. The right to receive information from the other parent concerning the health, education and welfare of the children;
2. The duty to inform the other parent in a timely manner of significant information concerning the health, education and welfare of the children;
3. The right to confer with the other parent to the extent possible before making a decision concerning the health, education and welfare of the children;

4. The right of access to medical, dental, psychological and educational records of the children;

5. The right to consult with a physician, dentist or psychologist of the children;

6. The right to consult with school officials concerning the children's welfare and educational status, including school activities;

7. The right to attend school activities;

8. The right to be designated on the children's records as a person to be notified in case of an emergency;

9. The right to consent to medical, dental and surgical treatment during an emergency involving an immediate danger to the health and safety of the children; and

It is ordered that, during their respective visitation periods, John Doe and Mary Doe, as joint custodians, shall each have the following rights and duties:

1. The duty of care, control, protection and reasonable discipline of the children;

2. The duty to support the children, including providing the children with clothing, food, shelter and medical and dental care not involving an invasive procedure;

3. The right to consent for the children to medical and dental care not involving an invasive procedure;

4. The right to direct the moral and religious training of the children.

It is ordered that John Doe, as a joint custodian, shall have the following rights and duty;

1. The right to consent to medical, dental and surgical treatment involving invasive procedures and to consent to psychiatric and psychological treatment of the children;

2. The right to represent the children in legal action and to make other decisions of substantial legal significance concerning the children;

3. The right to consent to marriage and to enlistment in the armed forces of the United States;

4. The right to the services and earnings of the children;

5. Except when a guardian of the children's estates or a guardian or attorney ad litem has been appointed for the children, the right to act as an agent of the children in relation to the children's estates if the children's actions are required by a state, the United States or a foreign government; and

6. The duty to manage the estates of the children to the extent created by Petitioner, John Doe, or his family; Petitioner shall continue to manage the trust containing real property at no expense to Respondent.

It is ordered that Mary Doe, as a joint custodian, shall have the following rights and duty:

1. The right to consent to medical, dental and surgical treatment involving invasive procedures and to consent to psychiatric and psychological treatment of the children;

2. The right to receive and give receipt for periodic payments for the support of the children and to hold or disburse these funds for the benefit of the children;

3. The right to represent the children in legal action and to make other decisions of substantial legal significance concerning the children;

4. The right to consent to marriage and to enlistment in the armed forces of the United States;

5. The right to the services and earnings of the children; and

6. The duty to manage the estates of the children to the extent

created by Respondent, Mary Doe, or her family; Petitioner shall continue to manage the trust containing real property at no expense to Respondent.

It is ordered that the primary residence of the children shall be in XXXXXX County or a county contiguous thereto ("Domicile area") and the parties shall not remove the children from the Domicile area thereto for the purpose of changing the primary residence of the children until modified by further order of the court of continuing jurisdiction or by written agreement signed by the parties and filed with the court. It is further ordered that John Doe shall have exclusive right to establish the children's primary residence within the Domicile area.

Most joint custody agreements contain language like this, with modifications to fit the everyday life of the children and the parents.

THE HOT TOPIC OF RELOCATION

One of the raging issues in jurisdictions across the country is whether divorced parents can remove the children from a certain county or state. For example, the Alabama State Legislature recently passed a law that requires the noncustodial parent to be notified when children are being relocated outside the state or more than 100 miles away. The parent without custody can then file suit against the parent instigating the move and use that action as a reason to contest custody. Statutes like these have been passed or are being considered in many states. These laws bring into conflict two fundamental rights. The first is our constitutional right to move freely within the borders of our country. The other is a child's right of access to both parents.

This is a highly controversial area that's virtually guaranteed to wind up in a blizzard of court actions and is subject to change through legislation or court order at any time.

Joint Legal Custody Language

The following language appears in divorce decrees in jurisdictions where decision making is left for the two parties to work out.

The parties hereby agree that they shall have joint legal and physical custody of the minor children pursuant to XXXXXXX, as amended. Husband and Wife both express their love and affection for the children born of this marriage, and each parent individually, and the parents collectively, desire to create an environment conducive to the children's best interests and one that adequately provides for their needs and welfare. This paragraph is intended to promote the love and affection of both parents for the children. The parties shall consult with each other regarding major decisions concerning the children's education, medical care, religious upbringing and general welfare. In the event the parties cannot agree regarding a major decision, XXXXXX shall act as a binding arbitrator of any said disputes. In case of an emergency, the party with the minor children in his or her present physical custody shall be the decision-maker with respect to medical emergency issues.

Each party shall exert every reasonable effort to maintain free access and unhampered contact between the minor children and the other party and to foster a feeling of affection between the minor children and the other party. Neither party shall do anything which may estrange the minor children from the other party or injure the minor children's opinion as to the Wife or Husband, or which may hamper the free and natural development of the minor children's love and respect for the other party.

JOINT PHYSICAL CUSTODY

A document that spells out physical joint custody is far more detailed than the one above. Similar language is part of an effective parenting plan in some southern states because it leaves less for the parties to discuss and agree upon. The text of a physical joint custody agreement can be found in Appendix C.

CUSTODY: THE BATTLE OF YOUR LIFE

When parents fail to agree on co-parenting arrangements, families sometimes wind up in nasty custody battles. There are many reasons why divorcing parents challenge each other for custody of their children. Pride often enters into it. Revenge is a motive in some cases. There is a streak of individualism that asserts itself in many of these instances. Parties decide they just aren't going to let someone — someone like a former mate — push them around. They want their day in court.

Money is an increasingly major factor in custody battles. The child support guidelines of most states now require substantial support payments from the noncustodial parent. If there are several young children when the divorce takes place, the parent without custody may be looking at a lifetime of significant payments. Faced with this prospect, many parents decide to roll the dice and attempt to gain custody themselves, so that they can make the important decisions on how money is spent on their children.

Sometimes, a parent doesn't really want custody, but he or she makes custody an issue to soften up the opposition for a run at more of the marital assets. Most of the time, though, parents contest custody because they sincerely believe the children are better off living with them rather than the other parent.

Each child custody case is unique due to the facts, circumstances and fault surrounding the breakup of the marriage, as well as each parent's individual relationship with the children during and after the marriage. A parent's role with the children after the divorce usually mirrors the relationship that parent had with the children beforehand.

If the marriage was set up in a traditional manner, with a working father and a stay-at-home mom, the father may have spent less time with the children than his wife did prior to the divorce. In such cases, he might not instantly become heavily involved in the children's lives, although there are exceptions. Statistics show that on average, men do better financially after a divorce than women. There are many reasons for this. One could be that men dedicate themselves to their work while women have to shoehorn work into the time between caring for children and vice versa. Common sense indicates that as more men gain custody of their children, the income disparity will decrease.

In a two-wage-earner family, both mother and father probably had work conflicts during the marriage that led to absenteeism at home. During and after the divorce, this pattern will probably continue. In some cases, there is a period of intense activity as one of the parents tries to make up for a prior lack of participation in the children's lives. He or she quickly becomes a "Disneyland" or "party time" parent.

No matter what caused the divorce, the children should not be made to feel that it was their fault and they should not be punished for the breakup. They deserve to have the best possible relationship with both parents after the divorce.

This means that in almost every jurisdiction, each parent will get significant time with the children except when there is evidence that one parent is a dangerous person.

Emerging from the process emotionally intact is essential to a successful divorce. It is in the best interest of the children for that to happen. It is also in the best interest of everyone for all parties to voluntarily uphold court orders or agreed-upon settlements. Statistics clearly indicate that the parent without primary custody is more likely to actually pay the child support ordered and help with other expenses if he or she sees the children regularly.

WHO SHOULD BE THE PRIMARY CUSTODIAN?

To be successful in a custody dispute, you must demonstrate that you are the primary custodian of the child. Often the parent who cared for the child during the marriage receives primary custody of the child after the divorce, unless there are significant conflicting circumstances or certain problems with that parent.

This is especially true with very young or pre-teen children. In most states, as children get older, their preferences are taken into account. In Texas, for instance, the court will take the opinion of a 12-year-old into consideration. At age 14, the child is allowed by law to choose which parent to live with.

To determine who has been the primary custodian of the young child, the courts usually consider who performs most of the following activities for the child:

Who helps the child get dressed for school?
Who fixes breakfast for the child?
Who packs the child's lunch for school?
Who helps the child with homework?
Who participates in school activities with the child?
Who takes care of the child after school?
Who bathes the child?
Who takes the child to the doctor?

Who takes the child shopping?

Who takes the child to religious activities?

Who arranges for the child's extracurricular activities?

Who helps the child in various stages of development?

Who nurtures the child?

It is also important for the court to know about changes that could take place in the household after the marriage. For instance, the mother might have been a homemaker during the marriage. When the divorce is final, she may be forced to work outside the home. The relative abilities of husband and wife to parent may be significantly altered.

WHAT A PARENT SHOULD KNOW ABOUT A CHILD BEFORE SEEKING CUSTODY

Here's a test you can give yourself concerning the care of your child. Any parent who has participated in the majority of the activities outlined above should be able to answer the questions below:

Who is the child's doctor?

Where is the doctor's office?

What allergies does the child have?

Who is the child's dentist?

Who is the child's principal?

Who is the child's teacher?

What is the child's favorite subject in school?

Who is the child's day care provider?

How often does the child go to day care?

Who are the child's three best friends?

What is the child's favorite book?

What is the child's favorite color?

What special needs does the child have?

What size shoe does the child wear?

What clothing size does the child wear?

Just because you don't know the answer to these questions today doesn't mean you can't learn them in a fairly short time. Often, a parent who means well has been involved in other facets of family life, such as earning money. If that person hasn't taken an active role in the child care, he or she needs time to learn these things about the child before being considered qualified to be the custodial parent.

One client was convinced his wife was mentally unstable and could not care for their children anymore. Although he worked long hours and traveled for his company during the marriage, he was determined to make a change. For months, he kept a journal of his wife's erratic behavior and learned the role of primary caregiver. After a disturbing weekend at home, the father's attorney filed the divorce. Because the man took on the caregiver role and could show how his wife's mental state was affecting his kids, he was awarded sole custody of the children and the wife received a safe amount of visitation.

USING CHILDREN TO GET REVENGE

"I always tell my son the truth. I think it is important that he knows his mother is a fat alcoholic." This straight-faced declaration by the father of a five-year-old speaks volumes about the visitation problems this divorced family will have in the future.

Young children especially can become entangled in their parents' problems with each other. No settlement agreement can address every circumstance that can arise in the raising of children. Disputes may involve the simplest of issues, from a parent who cannot pick up the child at a scheduled time due to unforeseen circumstances, to an important event the noncustodial parent refuses to take the child to during a visitation period.

Minor visitation problems get blown out of proportion. A client will occasionally telephone the attorney because an ex-spouse is 10 minutes late returning a child, and all hell will break loose between the parents. One judge reviewed such a case and asked the attorneys involved if their clients had lost their minds entirely. Why would any-one get the court involved over such a trivial violation of a court order? Had they never heard of a traffic tie-up or a wristwatch battery gone bad? The truth is that problems during and after divorce *are* magnified, sometimes beyond all reason. When a court order spells out a visitation schedule, some parents will take a zero-tolerance approach. Being late can be a form of rebellion for a noncustodial parent who is unhappy with the arrangement. And complaining about tardiness is a way for custodial parents to criticize the actions of an ex-mate.

Parents are not always allowed to take a child to sporting events, because the games are not during scheduled visitation. Even worse, the mother may tell the child she would like to let him or her go to the game, but she can't trust the father to get the child home on time. The child is denied an opportunity to be with the other parent and is placed in the middle of a visitation dispute. That child may even become fear-ful of the consequences when the visiting parent plans an outing and can suffer from various aches and pains because of stress.

STANDARD ACCESS

Courts try to stabilize children, sometimes at the expense of the parents' comfort, often by setting up a standard visitation order (called "standard access"). Some primary custodial parents have problems allowing the other parent to have even this minimum visitation with the children. But by establishing a specific visitation schedule, the courts attempt to diffuse visitation problems and ensure that children have access to both parents.

The court wants to foster the relationship of the children with the noncustodial parent. Unless you can prove that seeing this parent harms the children, usually the judge will not limit that parent's visitation to less than the standard access in your jurisdiction.

KEEPING PARENTS AND OTHERS IN CHILDREN'S LIVES

In most cases, children in a divorce deserve an equivalent amount of guidance from both parents. The children are entitled to have two parents who don't use them as pawns against each other. Parents may say they are just being honest with their children when they are simply trying to turn the children against the other parent by filling the children's heads with negative images.

One case involved a mother who talked so badly about the father all week that when it came time for his weekend visitation, the children didn't want to go with him. The mother said she could not understand why the children would not go. Eventually, it was shown that the mother said so many negative things about the father that the children truly believed he was a monster. The mother would give the children a tape recorder to record their father, since she believed he always lied to them. These children would pick up the phone when their father called and begin recording. Or they would turn the recorder on whenever he came to the door to pick them up. In this instance, the father actually was a fine person and a good father. When he sued for custody, the children testified that they loved their father very much, but they did not want to hurt their mother's feelings by going with their father. So they just didn't go on the visitation. The mother was found in contempt of court for willfully violating the court's order set forth in the divorce decree, and she was sentenced to jail. Occasionally, parents who act this way lose custody of their children. This mother not only taught the children to lie, but she also created a barrier that nearly destroyed the father's relationship with them. If not for the father's persistence, he would have been forced to give up on his children altogether.

This story illustrates the horrible way children can be used during and after a divorce. There are always differences of opinion over who is the better parent, but those disputes should be solely between the parents.

Lawyers who bring a child to testify in court merely to ask which parent he or she wants to live with are taking a huge risk with the well-being of the child and the viability of the case. It's a strategy judges won't often forgive, and it is frowned upon in most courts.

How much your children are harmed by a divorce depends largely on how you handle it. Your children will always remember this period in their lives. If you neglect them, they will never forget it. If you use them as pawns, they will realize it, today or in the future. One day, they will grow up and the games their parents played with their lives will become more apparent. The only winning course for a parent is to do what is in the best interest of the children.

Figure 3:
Criteria Used By Courts
To Determine Child Custody

State	Guidelines Part of State Law	Child's Wishes	Joint Custody Available	Cooperative Parent	Domestic Violence In Home	Health of Parent
Alabama	X	X	X		X	
Arkansas					X	
Florida	X	X	X	X	X	X
Georgia	X	X	X	X	X	
Kentucky	X	X	X	X	X	X
Louisiana	X	X	X		X	
Mississippi	X		X			X
North Carolina		X	X		X	X
Oklahoma	X	X	X	X	X	
South Carolina		X	X	X	X	X
Tennessee	X	X	X	X	X	
Texas	X	X	X	X	X	X
Virginia	X	X	X	X	X	X

Source: Excerpted from Chart 2: Custody Criteria, Family Law Quarterly, Volume 37, No. 4, Winter 2004. Copyright 2004 by the American Bar Association. Reprinted by Permission.

13

Supporting Your Children

The history of child support is one of side deals and negotiations, where the parties wind up in disputes over who owes what to whom. Consider the young divorced mother of two and her ex-husband. Ever since their divorce three years earlier, the father of their son had paid $500 a month in child support.

"They let me go," he told his ex-wife, about his job as a manager for a trucking firm. "I don't have the money to pay you."

The young mother wondered how she would make ends meet, but she didn't want to fight with him. "Okay, just pay me $100 a month for now," she told him.

The man was unemployed for two years, but through a series of odd jobs he was able to pay the $100 a month. When he returned to his normal profession, the checks for $500 begin to arrive again. That was fine, said the woman, but what about the money he was short during the two-year period of unemployment? In her mind, she was owed almost $10,000 in back support.

The man interpreted the agreement to mean that his ex-wife excused him entirely from paying the full amount. To the woman, it was only a temporary reprieve from his obligation. He didn't have the modification in writing, but he was honestly out of a job. He didn't have the money, but she needed it for their child.

Agreements like this, reached outside the judicial system, can cause resentment and ill will between the parties.

CHILD SUPPORT COLLECTION

An effort has been made in the last two decades to formalize the collection of child support, making this vital function more efficient and harder to avoid. Child support is the most overlooked and underpaid debt in our society. When welfare reform was passed in 1996, it was predicated on the idea that people could get off welfare much easier if parents who owed child support simply paid their fair share. All across the country, more than $34 billion in child support is owed from one parent to another.

In response to federal law, every state has established a child support enforcement agency empowered to help collect the money. In many instances, the first step in the collection process is finding the delinquent parent. The federal government has created the Parent Locator Service to harness the resources of the Social Security Administration and the Internal Revenue Service to locate a nonpaying parent or his or her employer. Once the parent is found, the custodial parent or the state can enforce a child support order signed by the judge and collect unpaid support. The law also permits the IRS to pay child support arrears from tax refunds the nonpaying parent may be owed by the government.

Many truly deadbeat parents not only move around a lot, but also have a hard time keeping a job. When the parent does work, a number of states allow the court to order his or her employer to make direct payments to the custodial parent from the wages of the supporting parent.

Some jurisdictions also fund local child support registries to receive court-ordered child support payments and forward them to the parents who are owed them. Supporting parents pay a small fee to have a record made of their payments and have the checks forwarded. This method provides evidence for court hearings when ordered payments are not made or when custodial parents attempt to punish their exes by denying that they ever received the payments.

SUPPORT PERCENTAGES DIFFER BY STATE

At one time, state laws left the awarding of child support to the discretion of the judge, who had to estimate the level of support the child needed and the parent could pay. But as the states began to construct a more formalized child support system, each state adopted guidelines designed to help judges with calculations and give parents some idea of what to expect.

Today, in most jurisdictions in the South, a child receives support until age 18, marriage or death, whichever comes first. Child support guidelines are based on the number of children being supported and a percent of the paying parent's resources or income. In one state, a parent of one child may pay 20% of net resources while the same parent may pay 30% of net resources for three children. Say this person makes $3,600 per month in gross monthly wages. Typically, he can subtract such expenses as taxes, union dues and health insurance to arrive at his net monthly resources of $2,700 per month. With three children, he would pay 30% of net resources, or $810. In some other states, such as

Georgia, child support is based on gross income. Some child support guidelines contain a chart similar in format to the Federal Income Tax chart that increases with the parents' income. Other states simply publish the percentages and rely on parents or judges to do the math.

Health insurance is a special concern of child support advocates. Depending on the state, the paying parent either provides the children with health insurance, in addition to child support, or receives a credit toward support by paying for this benefit. Some state family codes even specify how health insurance should be purchased or kept — through an employer or a separate policy — and add that if the parent chooses not to provide coverage, he or she is liable for the children's medical expenses beyond any insurance benefits available.

Support Addresses the Child's Needs

Disagreements often emerge about who benefits from child support payments. Let's look at the most traditional custody arrangement and how child support affects it. This would be a sole custody arrangement with the children living with the mother and visiting the father on a standard visitation schedule.

Because the mother in this scenario is the custodial parent and the children spend most of their time with her, at her place of residence, eating her food and wearing clothes she has bought for them, the father pays child support.

The vast majority of noncustodial parents understand that their support payments take care of some basic needs for the children. Some paying parents resent the payments because they must be made directly to the other parent and they cannot spend the support payments on the children themselves. Some refuse to pay because they see it as just another form of alimony.

But even with the most agreeable former couples, the basis for child support can be clouded by complex parenting arrangements or the presence of extraordinary wealth in the marriage.

Taking the traditional custody arrangement described above as a baseline, how would the amount of child support change with more-than-standard visitation by the noncustodial parent? What if the parents share joint legal and physical custody? What if the mother has inherited wealth and the father operates a forklift in a warehouse? What if the father has sole custody and the mother has to pay support?

Over the past two decades, courts in all states have worked to become less biased toward one gender or any proscribed method of finalizing child custody and support orders.

In North Carolina, for instance, the family code lays down no hard and fast rules about these often-difficult matters. The terms "sole" or "joint" custody have no special meaning in the state's law except the meaning divorcing couples give them in an agreement or the judge gives these terms in a court order. Without a written agreement or court order, each North Carolina parent has equal rights to the physical possession of children.

Divorcing parties with high incomes and numerous assets follow rules that can be different from those described elsewhere in this chapter. In most states, there is a ceiling on the amount of monthly income used in child support calculations. For instance, the guidelines may only reflect the amount of support possible with the first $6,000 of monthly income. If the paying party makes more than $6,000 per month, the court can look at the income and assets of both parties and the needs of the children to determine if additional child support is warranted. This allows the judge to use his or her discretion to set support.

Another common variable is the amount of visitation allowed, especially in the case of parties having joint custody. If the mother and father have substantially equal assets and the children alternate living one week with one parent and one with the other, child support guidelines might not be applicable.

It is understood that payment of child support should not be linked to how much visitation a parent receives. The parent receiving child support cannot deny visitation to a parent who misses child support payments, and the paying parent cannot withhold child support due to visitation problems.

That's how the law reads, but these situations arise anyway through vindictiveness, petty behavior or ignorance of the law. Sometimes, they cause parties to risk contempt of court. And in some jurisdictions, they can earn the offender a night or two in jail.

POST-MAJORITY COLLEGE SUPPORT

One of the few expenditures that continues beyond the age of majority is for specific college and other education-related expenses. When state laws address this situation, they either require parents to pick up these expenses or make that a matter for negotiation.

Alabama, for instance, requires parents to provide for a child's college education. The parents may never have gone to college. No one in their families might have attended college. But state laws mandate a provision for college expenses if the child wants to go and is academically able.

Support can be awarded beyond age 19, the age of majority in Alabama, to pay specific college and other education-related expenses such as tuition, books, room and board and fees. The parties can agree to other expenditures such as fraternity or sorority fees and the upkeep on an automobile, but the court usually will not require a parent to pay for these items.

Tuition expenses are based on in-state costs at public institutions. Scholarships are credited against these expenses. If college support begins before the children reach majority, the amount of child support being paid usually is reduced.

Most settlement agreements specify that one parent will pay all the college expenses. Usually, this is the same parent who pays regular child support. Or the parties can divide the expenses between them. If the parent with custody is providing college support, that fact is often used to argue for more alimony. ("I should receive more alimony because I have to support these children through college.")

When the children are so young that college expenses are too far in the future for planning, Alabama courts can "reserve the issue," allowing the custodial parent to come back to court and ask for these expenses at a later date. There are requirements that the child make acceptable grades and be making progress toward a degree to keep getting the money.

This type of college support is a hot-button issue being contested in the few states where it is the law. Many people believe that since a parent cannot be required to pay for college in an intact marriage, how is it constitutional in a divorce? This provision is certain to be challenged all the way through the court system. A more common approach to college support is to address the payment of college expenses in the divorce settlement. In most states, the courts cannot order parents to pay these expenses, but the parties may agree to provide the support.

Settlement agreements should specify which expenses will be paid by which parent. If, for example, a child wants to attend a particular private university, the agreement should specify the school and the anticipated cost, to avoid confusion in the future.

Figure 4:
Child Support Guidelines:
What's Included and Deducted

State	Income Share	Percent of Income	Medical Care Deduct.	Childcare Deduction	College Support	Shared Parenting Offset
Alabama	X	X	X	X	X	
Arkansas		X	X	X		
Florida	X		X	X		
Georgia		X	X	X		
Kentucky	X		X	X		
Louisiana	X		X	X		
Mississippi		X	X	X		
North Carolina	X		X	X		X
Oklahoma	X		X	X		X
South Carolina	X		X	X	X	
Tennessee		X	X		X	X
Texas		X	X	X		
Virginia	X		X	X		X

Source: Excerpted from Chart 3: Child Support Guidelines, <u>Family Law Quarterly</u>, Volume 37, No. 4, Winter 2004. Copyright 2004 by the American Bar Association. Reprinted by Permission.

14

Taxes and Insurance

There are no intrinsically southern approaches to the issues of taxes and insurance during a divorce or afterward. Even though some income tax and insurance rules are state concerns, they don't really have a regional character. But they are so important to a successful divorce that I feel compelled to include them here.

In times past, the paternalism of the Old South might have kept tax and insurance issues a secret from the woman in the marriage. But times have changed. More women are familiar with their family's overall financial details. And as I've mentioned before, court systems throughout the South are striving for gender neutrality.

DISCLOSING TAX LIABILITIES OR REFUNDS

How many times have we heard of one spouse or the other pocketing an income tax refund without the knowledge of the other? The practice is so common that many banks refuse to accept deposits made out to both spouses unless both of them are present or the depositing spouse has the other person's identification along with their signature on the check.

Divorcing couples can only file a joint federal income tax return for a particular year if they were married the entire year. Tax liabilities or refunds should be considered in any settlement agreement. Language should specify who is responsible for a deficiency assessment or how any refund will be divided.

In past years, spouses were required to satisfy tax liabilities incurred on their behalf, even if they were unaware of the deficiency. Internal Revenue System reforms in 1998 exempted certain "innocent spouses" from payment of tax bills due to the actions of an ex. Your attorney or accountant should be able to advise you on these matters.

WHO GETS CHILD TAX EXEMPTIONS?

Deciding which parent receives tax exemptions for the children is an important element of a settlement agreement. Most often, the primary custodial parent is automatically entitled to claim income tax exemptions for any children.

But one parent might use the exemptions as a bargaining chip in settlement negotiations, trading them for other assets. For example, a parent who is not working or makes less money than the other parent might not value the exemptions as much. Exemptions are most valuable to the parent who makes the higher income.

There is a level of income, though, where the higher wage earner loses the benefit of any exemption for the children, based on the Internal Revenue code.

Over the past decade, child support advocates have decried deadbeat parents who not only fail to pay what they owe, but also take the children as dependents on their taxes.

IRS form 8332 is used to release the claim to the dependency exemption after the divorce. This form must be executed to satisfy the IRS concerning exemptions in the future. You should consult with your lawyer or accountant in more detail about these issues to protect your interests.

CHILDREN'S HEALTH INSURANCE

Millions of children in this country are without health insurance. Many of them go without coverage because parents who are obligated to provide insurance fail to do so.

In some states, the parent obligated to pay child support is required to provide major medical insurance for a minor child. That obligation may be continued by agreement until the child graduates from college. In most cases, health insurance is available through the obligated spouse's employment. When that spouse does not have coverage provided in this manner, often he or she must purchase individual insurance for the child.

An important negotiation item is who pays for medical expenses that are not covered by health insurance. If health insurance is not available due to preexisting conditions or other factors, you might be on the hook for the total expenses of an illness or injury. Even when the child is covered, those expenses not paid by the insurance company can be substantial and include the deductible, copayments or other extraordinary charges for doctor, hospital, medical, prescription drug, optical, dental, orthodontic or other medically related expenses.

This issue should be thoroughly considered, because medical expenses associated with children can be monumental. If a child is diagnosed with a major illness, these expenses can be devastating and could force a parent into bankruptcy.

HEALTH INSURANCE FOR YOUR SPOUSE

Most health insurance plans will not allow one spouse to provide coverage for the other after the divorce. A spouse needing coverage often has one or more of the following options:

Coverage through an employer – You may not have selected this coverage before the divorce because it isn't the best coverage or it may be at a high price, but at least it is available and usually more affordable than the other solutions below.

COBRA (Consolidated Omnibus Budget Reconciliation Act of 1985) – If an employer plan discontinues your coverage, this federal program provides coverage for a limited time. The plan is administered through the employer and should offer the same benefits as the employer plan at a slightly higher premium. Each spouse should confirm that this type of coverage is available before final resolution of the case.

Individual plan – A spouse who is relatively young and in decent physical condition may qualify for an individual policy sold by a company representative or insurance broker. Usually, these policies are more expensive and offer less coverage than group plans.

State risk pool – Many states offer health insurance for people who cannot obtain coverage because of preexisting conditions or other factors. These plans are highly restrictive and many have long waiting lists.

If one spouse has a major pre-existing condition such as cancer or heart trouble, this condition may not be covered by the new insurance following the divorce. This possibility should be examined after the divorce to assess the costs associated with medical care.

Cancer or other major illnesses can play a large role in a party's financial need due to the associated costs, as well as the limitations such an illness may place on the spouse's ability to earn a living. As a result, parties may wind up disputing the severity of health conditions due to the potential implications.

For instance, a husband may claim that an on-the-job accident injured his back, keeping him from working and, therefore, from paying child support. His wife may argue that he is not really injured, but is simply lying to escape his responsibilities.

The man's attorney may have to hire a physician to assess his condition. Expert medical witnesses are expensive. Such an investment is worthwhile only when a large amount of money is at stake. The man could significantly reduce the cost of such a move by getting all medical records related to the condition for his lawyer to review. Otherwise, the lawyer may have to subpoena the medical records at considerable expense.

REQUIRE LIFE INSURANCE

When there are children and the settlement includes child support and other expenses, insist on life insurance to cover the possibility that the obligated spouse could die. The spouse making payments should be required to maintain adequate insurance until all debts are paid.

The obligated spouse can be required to maintain specific life insurance policies for a specified dollar amount, for a certain time period, and name the spouse or children as beneficiaries while there is a financial obligation under the divorce agreement.

Protection for children, if one parent should die, is essential to a successful divorce. The settlement agreement should specify that the obligated spouse cannot modify the life insurance policies or diminish their value by taking out loans against them, pledging, assigning or otherwise reducing the amount. Sometimes, if children are involved, one spouse may require that a trust be established for the life insurance proceeds. Under a trust, the obligated spouse specifies a trustee — often the former spouse or a family member — who is required to use life insurance proceeds for the benefit of each child. When the children reach majority, the trustee usually is required to distribute the remaining money to them.

15

One Man's Junk Is Another's Treasure

As you move toward the end of your marriage, it is essential to determine what possessions you truly value from it and, therefore, what you want to retain. Do you have great sentimental attachment to your home? Do you relish a split of your spouse's retirement accounts, just because you know that will cause the greatest upset? Or can you take a practical approach by accepting the maximum amount of assets, without regard to anything but value?

What one person *must* have from the marriage, another might not value at all. It sounds clichéd, but I've actually seen a settlement agreement hung up for weeks over possession of a piece of costume jewelry or a collection of music CDs.

The practical approach is always more productive and helps to facilitate a successful divorce.

Your attorney will help you determine the actual value of assets, minus the emotion. Some assets are worth a fight, while others are not. Here are the biggest financial mistakes people make when their emotions take over.

- They decide to hold on to the family residence, whether they can afford it or not. Homes are a large part of most marital estates. Dealing with them is so complex that we devote the next chapter to this subject.
- They forget that retirement accounts can and should be divided between the parties as part of a settlement.
- They fail to consider the debts in the marriage.
- They value closely held businesses incorrectly.

People make many other mistakes when feelings run their lives. They tend to forget that anything worth money is an asset, so they overlook the value of box seats or suites at sporting events, hunting leases and time shares, and even frequent flyer miles.

The greater of these mistakes can haunt you for a lifetime. More than 80% of people surveyed after a divorce believe they were robbed in the process. That means in many cases, both sides felt they were treated unfairly.

People feel cheated the most when they lose the power to make the decisions concerning their property, such as when the court has to decide the property settlement between two parties.

LEAVING YOUR FATE TO THE COURT

In this country, we pride ourselves on having the freedom to make our own decisions. Things can get dicey when we are free to make horrible mistakes.

You have this freedom at the beginning of a divorce. It is in your best interest to work out an amicable division of personal property before a judge has to do it. No judge wants to divide the highly personal items from a couple's life together, and so he or she will accomplish it quickly, as part of the resolution of the entire case. The court doesn't have the time or inclination to ruminate over the fact that you are fond of that armoire or that only you watched the flat-screen television.

You may take the time to detail what things mean to you, but a judge doesn't have the time to take such care.

COMMUNITY PROPERTY VS. EQUITABLE DIVISION

State law dictates the method used by judges to divide marital property. You either live in a community property state or one that employs the concept of equitable division to split property at divorce. The difference between the two is mostly nomenclature, whether property is divided "fairly" or "equally." There are 10 community property states and 40 that employ equitable division. Louisiana and Texas are the only community property states in the South.

Equitable division states tend to divide property fairly, basing that fairness on a number of factors. Community property states, however, presume to make an equal division of property. The difference between the two methods is subtle, but can differ greatly in the final outcome.

Equitable Division -- Factors considered by the courts in equitable division states include the length of the marriage and contributions of the parties to the marriage, both economic and noneconomic. The first step to dividing property in an equitable division state is to classify the property either as marital or nonmarital. Marital property is accumulated during the course of the marriage, without using assets owned before the marriage and excluding property acquired by gift or inheritance. Once the marital estate is determined, the court will make a division based upon equitable principles.

Community Property -- Judges in community property states begin by dividing all property into community property and the separate property of the parties. Separate property stays with the person who obtained it with separate funds or as a gift or inheritance, rather than by using community funds. Community property can be divided equally as a matter of law.

In both community property and equitable division states, questions arise about "commingling" of assets and income derived from separate property. Any income earned by the parties during the marriage is subject to division in both equitable division and community property states.

The two theories of property division may differ, but in practice they work pretty much the same. No matter whether the laws call for an equal split of community property or equitable division, the judge will often draw a line somewhere down the list of property to divide it. The division may be equal, but that often takes a back seat to just getting it done. If you don't get something you want, it may wind up on your spouse's side of the ledger. In a case like that, your only choices are to let it go or to trade something else of value that landed on your side.

This is the most common example of getting caught up in an ego war over property in a divorce. Even if you go to trial over more significant issues, such as the custody of your children or the ownership of a family business, try to work out the personal property division prior to trial.

Figure 5:
Factors Used to Determine
Property Division

State	Comm. Property State	Only Marital Prop. Divided	Factors Listed in State Law	Nonmonetary Contributions[1] Considered	Economic Misconduct[2] Considered	Contributions to Education[3] Considered
Alabama		X		X		X
Arkansas		X	X	X		
Florida		X	X	X	X	X
Georgia		X				
Kentucky		X	X	X	X	X
Louisiana	X					
Mississippi		X	X	X	X	X
North Carolina		X	X	X	X	X
Oklahoma		X		X	X	
South Carolina		X	X	X	X	X
Tennessee		X	X	X	X	X
Texas	X				X	
Virginia		X	X	X	X	X

Source: Excerpted from Chart 5: Property Division, Family Law Quarterly, Volume 37, No. 4, Winter 2004. Copyright 2004 by the American Bar Association. Reprinted by Permission.
1. Contributions to the marriage that may be work, but not money, such as housework.
2. When one of the parties abuses the marital estate.
3. When one spouse pays for a child's education.

16

Your Home – An Asset and More

T he late *Atlanta Journal and Constitution* columnist Lewis Grizzard knew a thing or two about divorce. He had been through several divorces himself. An author of humorous books, Grizzard may be best known among divorcing people for this line: "The next time I think about getting married, instead I'll just find a woman who hates me and buy her a house."

A TOP CONCERN

The Old South view of hearth and home as a preeminent concern of the family continues today. The home is the center of family life, the glue that often holds a family together. Besides having sentimental value, the home usually is the greatest single investment married couples will make and the largest portion of the net worth of most marital unions.

Here in the New South, homes are literally larger than life. The square footage of homes has increased dramatically in the past two decades. Many people live in houses so large and well appointed that they can barely afford the mortgage, taxes, insurance and upkeep with two people working and all the family's effort directed to paying for and maintaining the household.

Lending practices are designed to loan the amount of money an entire household can repay. Most two-wage-earner families buy the maximum amount of house they are qualified to buy. When a divorce takes place, the two people involved are left trying to provide for the home and another separate household along with the other expenses of a breakup. Often, the pressure proves too great and neither party is able to keep the home.

CAN'T PAY FOR THE HOME WITH EMOTIONS

Emotion often overcomes practicality when divorcing couples begin to negotiate what to do with the marital residence. At first, one or both of the parties feels he or she simply must retain the home with all its memories. This is where they raised their children. It's where they were once happy, and that's all they have at the moment.

When one side gains control of the home and realizes that times there weren't always so good, he or she may not want to live there after all. The high cost of keeping and maintaining the home can also hit them, and since they can't afford it, they decide to give it up.

Step back from the emotional tangle surrounding your home before you make a big mistake. Carefully examine your financial situation before you decide whether to pursue the home in the divorce settlement. Look at your income, plus the effect of child support or alimony payments, coupled with the debt each party must assume. It may be more practical to admit that you can't afford the house and, instead, set your sights on other assets.

Among the alternative ways you might deal with the residence are the following:

- Keeping the home for yourself, even if you have to give up other assets or struggle to maintain the home
- Selling the home and dividing the proceeds
- Transferring the home to your spouse for other considerations
- Transferring title to the home, then selling it
- Deeding the home to your spouse in exchange for a cash payment
- Setting up a Qualified Personal Residence Trust (QPRT)

Each method of dealing with the home is its own unique strategy.

KEEPING YOUR HOME

One of the parties could wind up with total ownership of the home as part of the overall property settlement. One of the biggest mistakes people make in the divorce is to base this decision on the emotional value of the home. By all means, seek the advice of a real estate professional about market values in your area and ask an accountant about tax implications.

Prepare a budget that includes the real cost of maintaining the home along with other realistic expenses to determine whether you can afford to keep the residence.

SELLING IT OUTRIGHT

If you agree to sell the home, how you sell the residence and divvy up the proceeds should be part of the settlement agreement. One party may receive all of the equity or the parties may divide it in some way, depending on the division of the other marital assets. The agreement must also spell out the tax consequences of the sale.

To give a ballpark idea of the property's value, you should have an appraisal done prior to sale. If the parties cannot agree on an appraised value, one way to solve the dispute is for each party to select an appraiser. These two independent appraisers select a third appraiser, who sets the value. No matter how many appraisers are part of the process, you will have to pay a fee to each one.

The appraised value is not always the final sales amount, but it does serve as an effective guideline when setting an asking price. The sales price is affected by fluctuations in the market and the demands of the parties. For instance, both parties may want a quick sale, so they can address other expenses. Often, a quick sale produces a lower selling price. You can decide the minimum sales price you will accept, but be realistic and flexible.

To make that sale happen, the parties select a broker or agent in the same way they choose an appraiser. The parties can select different agents and the two agents can select a third person who will handle the listing. Each broker or agent involved in the transaction is paid or receives part of the commission from the sales proceeds.

The settlement agreement should specify who pays the mortgage payment, taxes, insurance and utilities until the property sells. The party living in the house during the sale period should be required to provide routine maintenance and upkeep. And the agreement should address the responsibility for paying the cost of reasonable and necessary repairs — structural, heating, cooling, roofing and other maintenance items. Don't just leave this type of expenditure to chance, because the home's condition can affect the ability to sell the property and the final price.

Ultimately, the cost of those repair and maintenance items should be deducted from the proceeds at closing, unless one of the parties agrees to bear the cost. The following items should be deducted from the gross sales price before any money is distributed.

- Mortgage amount owed
- Brokerage commission
- Legal fees related to the sale
- Cost of repairs and improvements
- Applicable taxes and fees
- Other costs of sale
- Any other related terms of the settlement agreement, such as the payment of another debt

TRANSFERRING THE RESIDENCE TO YOUR SPOUSE

The settlement agreement should specify that when one party transfers interest to another, the transferring party loses any interest in the residence. When the settlement agreement is signed, the transferring party should execute a warranty or quit claim deed -— whichever is proper for your case and the jurisdiction — to make it official.

The settlement agreement should specify responsibility for the mortgage debt and address any tax consequences.

TRANSFERRING TITLE FOR A LIMITED TIME, THEN SELLING IT

A common arrangement is for one party to occupy the home for a specified period of time – until the party gets a job, finishes a training program or remarries, or a child graduates or reaches a certain age.

When that predetermined deadline approaches, the home is sold with the equity divided as specified in the settlement agreement. This option is often used when there are school-age children and the immediate sale of a residence would disrupt their lives.

Make certain the settlement agreement specifies how long the party can use the residence and what triggers a sale. Detail routine maintenance and upkeep, including the mortgage payment, and who pays for it. If your spouse stays in the home and you pay the expenses for an extended period of time, you may get the option to decide if the equity to be divided will be determined when the deal is struck or when the property is sold. Most homes appreciate in value over time, and you will probably want to take advantage of that appreciation.

DEEDING THE HOME IN EXCHANGE
FOR A CASH PAYMENT

This may be the simplest option. One party obtains full ownership of the home by paying the other party a cash payment at the time of settlement or in smaller payments over time. Be sure to deal specifically with the mortgage debt in the agreement and look at tax implications of the payout methods.

SAFEGUARD YOUR INTEREST

Before deciding what to do with your home, you have some homework to do. You should safeguard your interest in the home by the following:

• Discuss the home's value with a real estate agent. Just because your spouse says it is worth an amount doesn't make it true.

- Confirm that amount with an appraiser. I already outlined the appraisal process.
- Ask your lender about liability. If you are thinking about keeping the existing mortgage, find out the lender's policy about mortgage obligations. In most cases, both parties to a joint debt remain liable even if one transfers ownership to the other. The divorce decree may say you are not liable, but that doesn't affect the lender's position. If one spouse defaults on the mortgage, the lender usually comes after the other party.
- Do a title search. This is a simple search through county records to make sure your spouse doesn't have any liens or judgments against the property that would prevent a sale. The company that issued your original title policy can perform the search.
- Decide what you would do under the worst possible circumstances. If you lost a job or became seriously ill, determine if you could keep the house or what you would do if you couldn't. Don't let pride rob you of a place to live or the equity from your property.

STUDY THE TAX CONSEQUENCES

Meet with an accountant to analyze potential tax liabilities associated with the residence before determining what to do with the property. Under the Taxpayer Relief Act of 1997, you no longer have to worry about capital gains on the sale of a residence. Married couples who file taxes jointly may keep $500,000 in profits tax-free on the sale of a home they have owned and lived in for two of the past five years. Any profit above that amount is taxed at 20%.

17

You Can Divide Almost Anything in a Divorce

You might be a redneck if ... you've been involved in a custody fight over a hunting dog.

Jeff Foxworthy

In the Old South, they said no woman would come between a man and his truck, his dog or his shotgun. Atlanta resident Foxworthy became famous for lines like that on the network sit-com he starred in several years ago. He still gets big laughs on his Blue Collar Tour of concert halls all across the country. But the truth is that family courts across the South can surgically divide just about any asset.

These assets may include:

• Furnishings in the marital residence
• Bank accounts
• Stocks
• Bonds
• Mutual fund shares

- Checking and savings accounts
- Life insurance (whole or flexible premium policies with cash value)
- Retirement plans
- Individual retirement accounts (IRAs, Roth IRAs, etc.)
- 401(k) plans
- Stock options
- Business interests
- Patents and copyrights
- Jewelry
- Automobiles
- Antiques
- Family heirlooms
- Sporting equipment
- Artwork
- China, silver and crystal
- Boats and trailers
- Personal collections such as coins and stamps
- Gun collections
- Business equipment
- Tools
- Yard equipment

Personal property usually can be classified as follows:

- What each spouse brought into the marriage
- Property acquired by both spouses during the marriage
- Gifts and inheritances received by both spouses during the marriage (which may or may not be subject to division)
- Separate property purchased by both spouses during the marriage

Property must be classified, then that property classified as marital is divided. You can agree on a division of property or simply sell everything and split the proceeds. This is usually more satisfying than having a judge divide it.

If the parties cannot resolve the division of certain items, an acceptable alternative is the "me next" process of selection. The parties determine who will begin, and that person chooses one item from a list of disputed property. The other party goes next, picking an item from the list. The process is continued in turn until all items have been selected.

If one spouse wants to select the other's favorite item, the other spouse can return the favor with the next selection. This can be done item by item, by type of property, or room by room.

The final method of division, letting a judge do it, is the least desirable method. Judges do not have the time or patience to accurately balance the concerns of everyone over the division of personal property. How absurd is it to allow this complete stranger to decide who is virtuous enough to deserve the big-screen TV and who has to settle for the black and white set without a cable hookup?

Judges themselves admit they have shortcomings where the division of property comes into play. "I would not want a judge to decide personal property issues for me," says one circuit court judge. "Our knowledge of the history and facts of the case is too limited. For that reason, I have become a strong advocate of mediation, where the parties can take more time to expand on a solution than a judge can in a trial setting."

Most judges seek the parties' participation in the property division by requiring each of them to submit two personal property lists they consider a fair split. One party then selects one of the two lists provided by the other party.

To make sure one party doesn't get all the "good stuff" while the other gets very little, this method encourages the parties to spread out desired items between the two lists. With the major division accomplished, the parties may be able to negotiate the exchange of certain items because each will have bargaining chips for the negotiation.

COURT LOOKS AT MANY FACTORS

If the parties fail to agree, the court has no other choice than to split the property. In most jurisdictions, this happens in a very small percentage of cases. When it does, the judge needs some basis for making the division. He or she may ask the following:

- Who owns the property?
- Was the property owned prior to the marriage?
- Was the property purchased during the marriage?
- Was the property commingled during the marriage?
 (used for the benefit of both parties in the marriage)
- Did either party contribute money or labor to obtain the property?
- How long were you married?
- What are the parties' respective ages, health, occupation and ability to be trained for future employment?
- What is the degree to which a spouse has diminished his or her future earning capacity because of years spent caring for children?
- Does either spouse have the opportunity to acquire additional capital, assets or income in the future?
- What alimony payments will be made or received?
- What is the fault of each party for the divorce?

THE FAMILY BUSINESS

When married people own a closely held business or hold a substantial business ownership interest together, it is often the largest single asset in the marriage. They must decide how to handle the business as part of the divorce. Since this may be their most valuable asset, how the business is dealt with can be the most crucial decision to a successful breakup.

The settlement agreement at the end of the marriage should specify the following:

- The overall value of the business or business interest
- Which party receives the business
- How the business will be managed
- How the assets and debts of the business will be divided
- How the party who doesn't receive the business will be compensated

The process of answering all these questions begins by determining the legal form of the business and who legally owns it. The business may be in the name of one spouse, owned by both spouses, or owned by one spouse in a corporation, partnership or joint venture with other people or entities.

Sole proprietorships are the easiest to divide, while partnerships are more difficult and interests in corporations are the most cumbersome to split between two parties.

Even when one party is listed as the business owner and the other is not a regular employee, that other spouse may contribute to the success of the enterprise.

Quite often, when a business is in its infancy, a spouse who is not the business owner may provide free labor or fill in for employees who are ill or on vacation. The judge often takes into consideration that this spouse builds up sweat equity by enabling the spouse who runs the company to concentrate on attracting business.

WHAT'S THE BUSINESS WORTH?

Determining the value of the business can be the most significant disagreement in a divorce. The one who wants the business will give it the lowest possible value. Then, if that spouse has to pay the other one half the value, that amount will be minimal. The story may be that sales have headed downward or a new product has failed or some other factor has hurt the value. The spouse who doesn't want the business but wants the greatest possible amount of cash from it, only sees how lavishly the firm has provided for the family over the past years.

Here is one area where accepting the opinion of your spouse may cloud your future. An audit of business records may be necessary to determine the company's worth. At the very least, your attorney should examine tax returns and other corporate documents, including profit and loss statements and records used to secure financing. In more complex cases, a business appraiser will use the following information to form his or her impression of the value:

- The nature and history of the business
- Its tangible assets
- The earning capacity of the business
- Fair market value of all assets
- Amount of goodwill with customers and suppliers

In some large-asset divorces where business interests are extremely complex, both sides will hire business experts who present their theories and opinions on the value of a business. When those values are vastly different, the court has to determine which value is correct, based on the approach taken by the business appraisers. At other times, the court will simply split the difference and set the value between them.

RETIREMENT ACCOUNTS

Since the 1990s, when the asset totals of most family estates were fattened by various types of retirement accounts, divorcing couples have come to know the acronym QDRO ("Quadrow"). In 2000, the average 401(k) balance was $49,160, while the typical family with traditional individual retirement accounts held $85,600 in them.

Under a Qualified Domestic Relations Order, a spouse who amasses a sizable retirement account during the marriage may have to share it with a departing spouse. Because of the emphasis on retirement savings in tax-deferred accounts during the last decade, these investments sometimes are the largest assets in a marriage.

The QDRO is a specifically-written document that provides benefits for each party to the divorce. The owner of the 401(k), Keogh or other qualified plan is insulated from paying taxes on dollars transferred to a former spouse. The person who doesn't own the account can receive as much as half the value of the account.

Before signing off on a QDRO:

- Examine all retirement accounts. If your spouse is the plan member, you may have to get authorization or a subpoena.
- Don't assume the full value of a defined benefit is reflected in the statement. Verify that no significant withdrawals have been made just prior to settlement.
- Base your share of benefits on what will accrue at retirement, not when the divorce is final.
- If you are not the plan member, demand cost-of-living adjustments, early retirement incentives and survivor benefits. If survivor benefits are not addressed in the QDRO, all benefits could be discontinued when the plan member dies.

• The spouse who doesn't own the account is subject to the age and benefits due the other side. Find out what age the plan member must be to tap the benefits.

• Have your QDRO approved by the court and plan administrator before the divorce is final. The other side may have no real incentive to agree to anything after the fact.

Both sides will want to determine the value of the retirement account at the time of marriage and at the present time, and project a value at the time the account owner plans to retire. The plan's value at the time of the marriage is important because contributions before this time may be separate property and those during the marriage may be marital property.

Taking early distributions or borrowing from a retirement account can be done without severe financial penalties only in special circumstances. Check with an accountant to find the safest method to access these funds.

MONEY IN UNUSUAL PLACES

Wherever a person can conceive of stashing money and conveniently forgetting it, you should look for marital property hidden by your spouse. Some of the assets people tend to overlook are:

• Military benefits
• Stock options
• Social security benefits
• Season tickets and/or suites boxes at sporting events
• Frequent flyer miles
• Time shares

- Tax prepayments
- Gifts to friends and family members
- Offshore bank accounts
- Sale of assets at less than market value

You and your attorney should discuss the possibility that these assets exist and how likely you are to find them. But be prudent. Don't spend more money trying to uncover an asset than the asset could possibly be worth.

18

Taking on the Debts

If you could split up the assets in a marriage and toss out the debts, divorce would be a much more pleasant experience. Since your creditors are not likely to agree to that, the best approach may be for each party to take responsibility for the debts in that party's name and for both parties to pay off obligations in both their names.

Under this scenario, you would no longer be left holding the bag when your ex-spouse reneged on a debt. You are not off the hook even when a court says the opposing side should pay the balance on a credit card in both your names. Federal laws governing consumer credit supersede the divorce laws of your state. Until the balance is paid, the creditor will come after you.

How to Apportion Debt

Responsibility for debt in the marriage is determined by a variety of factors. Depending on the jurisdiction, it can include one or more of the following:

• Whose name is on the contract, invoice or credit card receipt establishing a certain debt
• The purpose of the debt
• Who retains the asset related to a debt
• Financial resources of the parties
• Any agreement, even an informal one, made by the parties
• Overall apportionment of assets in the settlement agreement
• Length of the marriage
• Fault of the parties

Compiling this information is a tedious job, but it must be done. And you are the person to do it. This information should include the names and addresses of creditors, as well as account numbers.

WHICH DEBTS ARE WE TALKING ABOUT?

You would think that settlement agreements always clearly specified which debts belong to whom, but you would be wrong. I've seen language in the agreement detailing responsibility for debt that is vague or indecipherable. An ambiguous agreement is impossible to enforce when the terms are not spelled out.

WHO'S LIABLE FOR A SPECIFIC DEBT?

Look at each debt as your own obligation, unless it has been specifically assigned to the other party. Even then, an unpaid debt after the divorce can come back to haunt you. Family courts have no authority to order a creditor to release one of its customers from liability.

If your ex does not make the prescribed payments, depending on the jurisdiction, your only recourse may be to take him or her to court on a contempt action. The creditor will still seek payment, but you might be able to secure a judgment or some recognition that the debt is not yours.

CHECK YOUR CREDIT REPORT

Don't sign a settlement agreement that says each of you will pay the debts listed in your name without verifying those accounts with the three major credit bureaus. Unless you have done an exhaustive review of your credit history, you may not know all the debts listed in your name. Your spouse may have borrowed money in both your names without telling you.

Even if your spouse paid off the debts assigned to him or her, the manner in which those debts were paid can impact your credit rating during and after the divorce.

Example: Under the terms of a settlement agreement, a woman kept her car, while her husband was ordered to make the payments. The woman tried to use her car as security for a bank loan to consolidate debts, but she was turned down. Her husband had paid off the note on the car, but he was late on several payments. She didn't know the bank came close to repossessing the car more than once. Because of his delinquency, she was deemed a high credit risk and refused a loan.

BANKRUPTCY AND MARITAL DEBT

A spouse who declares bankruptcy after negotiating a settlement agreement can create havoc with the other party's credit. Just as creditors can come after you for money when your ex is late with payments, they can do the same if he or she declares bankruptcy.

If you are the one filing for bankruptcy protection, list your ex-spouse as a creditor if you agreed in the divorce to pay certain obligations and hold the other spouse harmless.

If the other party files, talk to your attorney immediately and declare your objection quickly. Certain rights are lost if you do not move to protect yourself.

The affect of a bankruptcy declaration is to discharge debts, especially those not secured by collateral such as real estate, automobiles or consumer goods. Unsecured debt associated with divorce, such as child support, alimony and certain maintenance payments, cannot be discharged in bankruptcy, and all property settlements are subject to a decision of the court.

In some states, a spouse who declares bankruptcy to get out from under a divorce-related debt can be ordered to pay a higher amount of alimony to the other spouse after the bankruptcy. Some states allow you to reserve some issues, not making them final, until you see if the other side follows through as agreed. The issue of alimony is one that might be reserved in some jurisdictions. This allows you a safety net in case the paying spouse defaults on debt obligations.

You might be better off taking a greater share of an asset and being responsible for insuring that debts are paid than leaving payment to a former spouse.

OTHER MEANS OF DEBT RELIEF

Bankruptcy is the most extreme remedy for financial problems following divorce, but there are alternatives.

If you receive the marital residence or other real property in the divorce, you may qualify for a second mortgage or equity line of credit. This money can be used to consolidate several debt obligations into one payment and often provide tax benefits. If you have a good relationship with a bank or other lender, you may be able to consolidate your debts into one manageable payment at a reasonable interest rate even without collateral.

Credit counseling agencies provide this service, also. The Consumer Credit Counseling Service (CCCS) is a nonprofit organization that offers a debt management program. For people with severe money troubles, CCCS helps you repay your debts by restructuring your budget and negotiating with your creditors. Several hundred CCCS offices across the South provide low-cost or free services.

19

Settling Temporary Matters

The first step after filing for divorce is to set the ground rules for the time before the divorce is final. This is an important period, and how you go about deciding temporary living and financial arrangements can determine the success of your breakup. After the divorce is filed, you and your spouse must answer the following questions:

- Where will the children live?
- Who will live in the marital residence?
- How much child support or spousal support will be paid?
- How will assets and bills be handled before the divorce is final?

In some jurisdictions, these questions must be dealt with in formal hearings, while in others these issues can be settled between the parties and their lawyers.

Temporary Maintenance

Spousal support is a temporary form of maintenance that can be ordered or agreed upon during the divorce. Temporary maintenance is meant to pay for the transition from one household to another. Usually, it is paid to the spouse with the most limited resources and with temporary custody of the children.

Temporary Custody

Parents often go to extraordinary lengths not to disrupt their children during a divorce. The parent with temporary custody of the children usually receives the house, but this isn't always the case. In some cases, the parties get creative with their living arrangements, agreeing that the children stay in the home while the parents alternate weeks living there with them. This can make for some crazy schedules at a stressful time, but it reflects the belief many parents have that keeping the schedules of their children as normal as possible is worth their own inconvenience.

Attorney Fees and Court Costs

A client may have a high net worth but little cash on hand. In marriages where the other party controls the purse strings, how to retain and pay your attorney during this time is a big question. Maintaining a tight rein on the money can be an effective strategy to control the situation, but most courts allow a party to petition for the money to pay an attorney and continue the divorce.

20

Alimony

One fact about alimony is consistent; in practically every case, the party paying it hates to write that check to an ex-spouse every month, and the party receiving alimony relishes the exercise. Nothing is more contentious than the issue of alimony, but it can be a helpful way to distribute the resources of a marriage without triggering the sale of assets by the paying spouse.

If one spouse wants to retain a large asset such as a family business, he or she may have to agree to periodic alimony payments that equalize the value of property each party receives in the marriage. Alimony can also be used to help a spouse establish a financial profile. The classic example of this is the wife who left the workforce many years ago to raise the couple's children and support the working efforts of her husband.

To qualify for a job that will earn her enough money to meet her financial obligations, this woman will have to go back to school or complete a training program that hones her competitive skills.

Since the South is joining the rest of the country in its attempt to become gender neutral in legal matters, this example also holds true for men when the woman is the dominant breadwinner. But the recipient of rehabilitative alimony is most often a woman.

EACH STATE LOOKS AT ALIMONY DIFFERENTLY

The Old South tradition of paternalism toward women has dissolved into a myriad of differences over the issue of alimony. Every state has a different take on the subject.

Alabama, for instance, has both periodic and rehabilitative alimony. One spouse can also make a single payment to the other as part of the overall settlement. This is alimony in gross.

But in Texas, one of the last states to establish alimony, few people qualify for alimony because the statute establishing it is written so narrowly. Alimony in Texas is strictly rehabilitative. Most who qualify for alimony in Texas are poor women, but the resources of their marriages are limited, and the husbands rarely have the money to pay alimony.

HOW THE COURT DECIDES

When courts in the South assess alimony, judges often look at the following factors to determine the payments:

- The parties' financial resources
- Length of the marriage
- The parties' respective ages, health, occupations and employability
- Apportionment of property under the settlement agreement
- Diminished earning capacity of one spouse after years at home
- Standard of living enjoyed during the marriage
- Tax consequences of alimony
- Fault of the parties

Figure 6:
Criteria Used By Courts
To Determine Alimony/Spousal Support

State	Factors Listed in State Law	Marital Fault Not Considered	Marital Fault Relevant	Standard of Living	Status as Custodial Parent Considered
Alabama			X	X	
Arkansas		X			
Florida	X		X	X	
Georgia	X		X	X	
Kentucky	X		X	X	
Louisiana	X		X		X
Mississippi			X		
North Carolina	X		X	X	
Oklahoma		X		X	X
South Carolina	X		X	X	X
Tennessee	X		X	X	X
Texas	X		X	X	X
Virginia	X		X	X	

Source: Excerpted from Chart 1: Alimony/Spousal Support Factors, Family Law Quarterly, Volume 37, No. 4, Winter 2004. Copyright 2004 by the American Bar Association. Reprinted by Permission.

21

When Couples Never Marry

One of the fastest growing demographic groups in this country is people who live together outside marriage. Even in the South, which has a history of repudiating such behavior, cohabitation is on the rise. In the past 40 years, the number of unmarried couples living together has increased almost 10-fold. Most of the people experimenting with these living arrangements are in their 20s and 30s. More than half of all first marriages take place after living together.

Sociologists and demographers, who often find a cloud for every silver lining, believe the recent flattening out of the divorce rate all across the country is merely a factor of fewer marriages. If people don't marry in the first place, they don't get divorced.

But if they live together outside traditional marriage and decide to dissolve their relationship, the effect can be even more destructive than actual divorce.

Dissolving a marriage may be troublesome, but it's a mess that's far easier to clean up than a relationship with no legal paper.

You can be misled by the casual manner in which cohabitation often begins. People sometimes wind up living together before they know what happened to them. With no planning going into the arrangement, rarely is any provision made for dissolution of the relationship.

Suddenly, one party leaves the other with the rent or mortgage payment due. What recourse does a person have in this situation, if the couple buys furniture together, shares a bank account or has a child?

STATISTICS: *Living Together*

Fourteen states and the District of Columbia recognize common law marriage. Those states south of the Mason-Dixon Line are Alabama, Georgia (if the marriage was created before 1997), Oklahoma, South Carolina and Texas.

- Vermont has the highest percentage of unmarried couples living together.
- Alabama has the lowest percentage of unmarried cohabitating partners.

States with laws (that are rarely enforced) making unmarried cohabitation illegal include Florida, Mississippi, North Carolina and Virginia.

- South Carolina has a law against "fornication."

Reprinted by permission from the Alternatives to Marriage Project, www.unmarried.org, 2003.

COMMON LAW MARRIAGE

This popular form of marriage in the early South was not a way to skirt conventional unions. In a land where judges and preachers were often unseen for months at a time, residents of rural communities often married under common law rather than waiting for official sanction.

This was a way to satisfy community moral standards without having to travel far away and interrupt their farm duties. As time passed and the South became more urbanized, conventional marriages were easier to obtain. Today, only five southern states are among the 14 states and the District of Columbia that recognize common law marriage.

Common law unions are more like conventional marriages than just living together. They are not created when two people simply live together for a certain number of months or years.

To validate common law marriages, the couple must do all of the following:

- Live together for a significant period of time, which is not defined in any jurisdiction
- Hold out to the public that they are married, typically by using the same last name, referring to the other as "my husband" or "my wife" and filing a joint tax return
- Agree to be husband and wife

In this way, being married under common law is not the simple commitmentless arrangement that many people have come to understand. It is far more binding than just living together.

Common law spouses have practically all the rights and responsibilities accorded formally married couples, including having to go through a legal divorce to end the relationship.

LIVE-IN ARRANGEMENTS

These are not as clear-cut as common law unions. In most cases, the agreements made are not part of family law, but are treated the same as contracts. Two people agree to do something – live together, rent or purchase a home, run a business, sell merchandise. It's all the same to the courts. If both parties do what they agree, that's fine. If one or the other fails to perform as promised, the case usually goes into the state's regular civil court system.

To be legally binding, each party must provide something of value. On a modest scale, the man might pay the rent while the woman cooks the meals and cleans the house. For wealthy professional people, the couple might use the man's house and car, while the woman provides public relations consultation to his company.

The couple must be dealing in good faith and the agreement cannot violate the law. Agreements in which one party essentially provides nothing but sex are, in most cases, against the law. Several high profile cases seeking "palimony" from rich or famous people were thrown out because, according to this interpretation, the services amounted to prostitution.

PROPERTY AND CHILDREN

Live-in arrangements have a way of evolving into something legally serious. It's precisely because the process is evolutionary that it can be so insidious. Relationships seem pretty harmless when one party simply leaves a toothbrush at the other's house. The person staying over gets a bathroom drawer and then a closet. The law only takes notice when people purchase property together or have children.

When two people buy a sofa together, they can decide which one keeps it and how much he or she will pay the other for half the value. In the case of the purchase of a business, the two parties might want to execute a partnership agreement with a buyout provision that is triggered if the relationship goes sour.

These situations get more complicated when unmarried people have children. The courts don't look at children as the property of either party. Judges usually consider the best interest of the children in determining where they will live.

As with children of conventional unions, custody does not always go to the mother. Fathers gain custody in some instances, as do grandparents. The man in the relationship is presumed to be the father and automatically has all the rights and duties of a parent if he consents in writing to be named on the child's birth certificate. It's best to settle the question of custody in a court order at the point of the breakup, so that it doesn't become an issue later in the child's life.

Between 1978 and 1996, the number of babies born to unmarried women per year quadrupled from 500,000 to more than two million. Today, one-third of all children are born to unmarried parents. Many of these children are subjects of custody battles, conflicts over visitation rights and child support enforcement fights.

PROVING PATERNITY MAY BE IMPORTANT

Statistics show over the years that children of unmarried unions receive far less child support than those from conventional marriages. In many cases, the fathers simply refuse to believe these are their children. Proving paternity is essential to getting child support in such instances. Each year, several hundred thousand paternity cases are filed in an effort to clear up ambiguities about parental responsibility. Blood tests in years past could prove that a man was not the father, but not that there was a positive match. Now, high-tech methods of DNA finger-printing can establish parentage to a 99% probability. Men who have been paying child support for many years are now finding out whether they are actually biological fathers. Numerous lawsuits have been filed seeking to terminate relationships, discontinue payments and seek refunds based on fraud principles.

Men who want to establish parentage when the mothers deny it can use the new technology as a basis to assert their rights.

22

Evaluating Your Attorney

Attorney Coyt Randal Johnston knows every unprofessional and inconsiderate thing divorce lawyers do to their clients. As one of the South's top practitioners in legal malpractice, Johnston hears the gripes clients have about those who represent them.

"Ninety percent of the people who come to me want to sue divorce lawyers," he says. "This could be because there are so many divorces, or because there are so many bad divorce lawyers. I don't know which one is true, but hearing all these complaints doesn't improve my image of family law practitioners."

Most complaints deal with money — exorbitant fees or the indiscriminate use of a client's resources by an attorney. Johnston knows that people are at their most emotional in the midst of a divorce. Because most people come to him with emotional bases for suits rather than factual ones, he doesn't take many claims against divorce lawyers.

But still the Dallas attorney knows that some of these lawyers "churn" fees by convincing a client that an action by the other side was egregious and should be fought, often at great expense.

Clients complain about the attorney behaviors already mentioned; that they don't pay close enough attention to their cases, don't return phone calls or fail to prepare adequately for court.

When things don't go their way and they lose either custody of a child or some asset that's important to them, clients have been known to accuse their attorney of selling out to the other side or being in collusion with the judge.

"Just because an attorney loses doesn't mean it's malpractice," Johnston says. "You may not have the facts on your side, or you and the other witnesses may not have presented yourselves well in court."

Johnston describes himself as "a traffic cop" who pulls over the very worst offenders among attorneys.

"They make it tough for the most ethical lawyers to do their job," he says.

GETTING THE MOST FROM YOUR LEGAL DOLLARS

In contested divorces, you may ask if you are getting your money's worth from your attorney. This evaluation of the legal skill working in your favor usually happens at one specific point; after the initial rush to gather information, after depositions and other discovery, often after the first settlement discussions and normally before the case goes to trial. Emotions at this point may be running especially high and you may not be thinking straight. Here are some benchmarks that will help you evaluate the quality of your legal counsel.

- Are you closer to resolving the divorce than you were when you hired your attorney?
- Consider what your attorney said to expect. Is it anywhere near the current situation, especially in terms of the assets you

should get and your arrangements with your children?

• Will you and your soon-to-be ex be able to deal with each other when the case is over?

• Is the divorce costing you more than the worth of assets you are going to retain?

The cost of a divorce is directly related to the way the attorneys conduct business and the passions you and your spouse bring to the proceedings. Did you, through word or deed, suggest that your lawyer engage in a slash-and-burn policy that inevitably uses up your resources as it gets the attention of the other party. If your objective was to aggressively punish the opposition, don't be surprised if nothing is left – no relationships, self-respect or money. Do you expect your attorney to report to you each time he or she engages in aggressive action? Or do you simply expect your attorney to demonstrate knowledge of your case and the law, prepare well and come equipped with a plan?

A small measure of realism in the face of this difficult situation can result in a more successful divorce.

WHAT'S YOURS DOES NOT BELONG TO YOUR ATTORNEY

A young man in a southern city conferred with an attorney about a custody case involving his only son. An essential part of the initial meeting was filling out a questionnaire for the attorney. The form included a couple of pages of information about the young man, his son and his ex-wife. There was also a place on the form for annual income, net worth and cash on hand.

"So, how much do you charge to handle a case like this?" asked the young man. The attorney shuffled through the pages, looked down at the section on finances and said, "At least $30,000."

It was the same amount the young man had written under cash on hand. The attorney probably thought he was accommodating himself to the young man's financial situation. For the young man, it was an indication that the attorney was going to get all the money he had.

Even very wealthy people will question exorbitant legal fees in a divorce case. Some attorneys invite these questions by a controversial practice known as value billing.

This type of billing assumes you will pay the attorney's hourly billing. But that's only the beginning. If the attorney does the job he or she was hired to do, the final bill will actually be much higher. Most of these arrangements based on performance are unofficial and depend on goodwill between the attorney and the client, but they are contingent on the idea that whatever money the attorney wins for the client, the attorney is entitled to a share in addition to an hourly fee.

Value billing is dangerously close to payment by contingency fee, the method most personal injury attorneys use for compensation. But payment on contingency is illegal in family law cases in most southern states.

Could This Be the Wrong Attorney For You?

Expectations play a central role in whether you remain satisfied with the performance of your attorney. If that person has a reputation for excellence or dazzles you from the start with claims of what he or she can win for you in the divorce, you will expect to walk away with everything and have fun doing it.

If your lawyer just passed the bar exam, has an office next to the firm's men's room or shrugs his shoulders when you ask what to expect from the litigation, you may be satisfied to emerge with your separate property intact.

Measuring results as the case progresses against the expectations you had at the start can give you a good idea if this is the correct attorney for you.

Attorneys are not all the same. One might be so wired that he or she yells at the firm's receptionist, while another is so laid back that Friday afternoons are for golf and not conferences with hysterical clients. One may have a sense of urgency that comforts you while others seem too distant and removed.

Style plays a big role in whether you are comfortable with your attorney. Good results seal the deal.

In essence, conflicts that clients have with their attorneys result from one or more of these three complaints:

- Your attorney doesn't return your phone calls.
- Your attorney stirs up trouble needlessly, using up the retainer money.
- The money you pay your attorney gets used, but nothing seems to get done.

YOUR ATTORNEY DOESN'T RETURN YOUR PHONE CALLS

The most common grievance against attorneys, in the South and throughout the country, is the lack of communication with clients. Attorneys are notorious for not returning telephone calls. Some don't call because there is nothing to report. Others do it because they don't want to give bad news. Still others take on so many cases at one time that they can't remember which client is which and what to communicate to whom.

In one of the most extreme cases, a divorce client hired an attorney and then couldn't get the attorney on the phone for months afterward. Occasionally, the client would get some paper in the mail from the attorney's office, but there was never any explanation of what it meant or where the case went from here.

Six months passed and the client was beside himself. He talked to the attorney's legal assistant, but she always referred his questions to the attorney. Finally, he fooled the receptionist into giving him the attorney's cell phone number, faked an emergency and confronted him in his car.

Without apologizing or even noting the client's displeasure, the attorney said things were happening in the case and he was on his way to the courthouse to deal with them.

"I was just about to call you because we have a settlement offer from the other side," says the attorney.

"What does it say?" asks the bemused client.

"I'm not sure," replies the attorney. "I haven't read it."

TOO ACTIVE FOR YOUR GOOD

Churning fees can be a part of the divorce lawyer's mode of operations. It works like this. The attorney recognizes that his or her client is very excitable and really wants to get significant points across to the other side. Wreaking a little vengeance along the way is a side bonus.

To accomplish this, the attorney suggests filing various motions, opposing certain temporary orders and generally papering the opposition in a way that causes inconvenience and expense. Some of these strategies may be productive parts of the attorney's conduct of the case, but most are meant only to waste motion and churn fees.

The worst thing a client can tell an attorney is, "I just want you to win. I don't care how much it costs."

One client, a physician, did just that. It was soon after that he emptied out his money market account to pay the attorney's retainer and get him on the case. It would be a complex divorce with two children and ownership of the medical practice at stake. The doctor was also incensed that his wife put up such a fuss about his affair with his nurse.

Soon the paper was flying in a divorce petition and numerous motions full of accusations and invective about his wife, the mother of his children. When the doctor called his attorney, there was no problem getting through. He engaged the attorney in long strategy sessions in which the client railed against his wife. He even called the attorney on the weekend, including calls to his cell phone and his lake house.

Soon the retainer was gone and the doctor had to replenish it. But the attorney was making things happen. Practically all the people affected by this divorce hated him. Friends were rallying around his spouse. His children were so traumatized that he had to begin paying for counseling. His practice began to suffer an unusually high number of appointment cancellations and the level of tension was so elevated that he had trouble sleeping.

He had enough, went to the attorney and laid out his complaints. The attorney had a different understanding. "You wanted me to spare no expense, be aggressive and make the other side miserable," the attorney responded.

The doctor was beside himself. "But I didn't ask you to make *me* miserable," he said.

The attorney's tactics had accomplished just that, and he was no closer to a resolution than before all the money was spent. This client eventually learned the hard way about winning at all cost. He resolved to sit down with the attorney and give him new instructions about handling the case in a constructive manner.

There would be no more panicky calls on the weekend. He would save up his questions and ask them of the attorney all at once. They would do their business, then get off the phone or end the meeting. Once the tension resided, the parties were able to settle the case.

HIRING A NEW ATTORNEY

Most attorney/client disputes are a matter of miscommunication. But sometimes people simply can't work together, no matter how hard they try. If you reach this point with your attorney, it may be time to find another. First, consider your motivation. Are you changing horses because you can't cross the stream or because the horse you've put your money on can't jump the unrealistically high barriers you've placed in front of him?

Changing attorneys without a good reason usually means you are the difficult one, not the lawyer. But if you have studied the situation and are determined to change, it should not be difficult to do.

Timing is an important consideration. If you make a change when you are facing an immediate court appearance, your new attorney may not have the time to prepare as well as the other side.

After you have checked the calendar for your case, call or write your lawyer and ask to have your file sent to you or to your new attorney. If you cannot reach your attorney by phone, send a fax and call the attorney's office to confirm that it was received. Or send a letter with return receipt requested.

When you terminate an attorney/client relationship, you must settle all money matters pending. If you owe the attorney money, request a bill and send a check along with your request for your file.

As consumer attitudes have affected the sale of legal services, numerous state bar organizations have made it illegal for attorneys to keep unbilled retainer money. Even in states where such financial arrangements are allowed, public perceptions and the threat of competition have made refunds a wise thing. Check the written fee agreement you signed when you hired your attorney. It should specify the necessary arrangements in case of a termination.

TOWARD BETTER ATTORNEY/CLIENT RELATIONS

The attorney/client relationship is like few others in our society. It melds the professional sensibilities of the attorney with the everyday wisdom of the client. The things you say to each other are privileged, which means that a court cannot compel either of you to disclose those conversations. And to be successful, the relationship must be based on trust. You, the client, must trust that the attorney knows what he or she is doing in terms of the law. And the attorney must trust that the client is being as truthful, and helpful, as possible.

The following are some general suggestions to help you get the most from the relationship with your attorney:

- Trust your attorney, or hire someone else.
- Make certain your attorney's goals for the case match yours. Don't just assume you are thinking alike.
- Recognize that your attorney usually knows best when it comes to the law.
- Help your attorney understand the layman's perspective on family law.
- If your attorney gives you homework, do it.
- Assist your attorney in preparations for the case.
- When your attorney communicates with you, respond quickly.
- Understand that your attorney has other clients who also demand time.
- Insist on itemized legal bills.

- Pay your legal bills promptly.
- Show up 15 minutes early for all appointments, hearings, depositions and court appearances.
- Help your attorney get witnesses and other important people to depositions and court appearances.
- Prepare yourself for the pressure of giving courtroom testimony.
- Follow your attorney's instructions during court proceedings.
- Offer your insight about witnesses, financial and other details.
- When the case is over, try to look at the outcome objectively.

Gentlemen, a court is no better than each man of you sitting before me on this jury. A court is only as sound as its jury, and a jury is only as sound as the men who make it up.

Atticus Finch,
***To Kill A Mockingbird*, 1960**

PART FOUR

When A Case Gets to Court

23

It's Not Criminal Law, But It's Still Serious

Just walking into a courtroom, either for a temporary hearing or a final trial, makes a person inexperienced with the setting feel he or she has done something wrong. It may only be a civil court — one that hears business lawsuits or domestic relations cases — but still you feel guilty of something and incredibly vulnerable. Except in rare instances, there is no jury for family law cases throughout the South. But there is a finder of fact, the judge, and you feel the presence of the law.

The harsh realities of the judicial system let you know this is serious business. There's no fooling around here. You must stay calm and collected to have control over the situation, rather than the court experience controlling you.

PREPARATION FOR TRIAL

In divorce, as with other facets of life, the one who is better prepared has the best chance of winning. How you look and act in the courtroom is important. Do you have witnesses and are they prepared? Does your theory of the case make sense?

Once your attorney becomes familiar with your rendition of events, collects financial information, interviews potential witnesses and absorbs everything else relevant to the case, it is essential for the two of you to review the entire case prior to trial.

Your attorney should tell you what will happen during a hearing, because it will affect the eventual outcome of your case. You should have the relevant issues explained to you. Your counsel may even request that you attend a trial similar to yours, so that you can get a good idea of the intensity of the proceeding and what to expect from the opposing counsel and the judge.

Preparation may include your lawyer running through the questions you might be asked and the best answers to those questions. No officer of the court should ever ask you to get on the stand and lie, but nowhere is it said that you must make the opposition's case for them by saying too much or venturing guesses on their behalf.

Here's an example: A client in a child custody case has a family history of high blood pressure and takes medicine to control his own blood pressure. He expects his wife's attorney to portray him as a severely ill person who cannot take care of their young son. But he has never been diagnosed with a heart condition and is a healthy, active man in his mid-30s.

If he is asked, "Do you take blood pressure medicine?," the answer is yes. Millions of people with children take this type of medicine. If the attorney asks, "Do you have heart disease?," the answer is an emphatic no. The client may wonder about the possibility that he has heart disease. Others in his family may have died of the disease. But it's a leap from controlling high blood pressure to being debilitated by heart disease.

It might be reasonable to speculate that this man's health could fail some decades in the future. But without solid evidence to the contrary, this man is healthy. If the question comes up at trial, this line of questioning seems like a needless invasion of his privacy and a complete waste of time.

You're Under No Obligation to Inform

You are paying your attorney to know how much or how little information a judge or jury needs to make a decision in your case. Many clients want to tell the court the most intimate details of who did what to whom. A good lawyer is acutely aware that time is precious in the courtroom. You can frustrate a judge or put a jury to sleep with repetitive or irrelevant details.

A litigator's job is much like that of a consultant to a political campaign. In almost every campaign, there are many issues and positions on those issues that a candidate can use to hone his message and convince people to vote for him. The consultant knows that you can't emphasize every issue. Some will resonate with the public, while people don't care about or understand others. Not every issue can be expressed on a bumper sticker or in a 30-second television commercial. The litigator, like the consultant, must select the issues that can easily be expressed and will be most effective.

If your lawyer wastes too much time listing your favorable attributes over and over again, the judge may become frustrated with your side for wasting his time. Once you establish that your spouse abused your children, don't give that spouse an opportunity to rehabilitate himself before the court, no matter how eager you are to tell the whole sad story.

You establish your case by answering questions from your attorney on the witness stand. When the other side asks you questions, your ability to tell your story is limited by the attorney doing the asking. Most of the questions the other attorney asks on cross examination can be answered "yes" or "no." You will only be allowed short answers. Even if you want to elaborate, the other lawyer will probably cut you off.

For instance, you may be asked, "Have you ever yelled at your children?" For most people, the answer is, "Yes, of course." You will want to explain the circumstances, but the attorney may not let you. Sometimes, the other lawyer attempts to frustrate you on purpose, so you lose your temper and show the judge or jury what a maniac you can be. Even the most genteel people lose control under difficult circumstances. A thorough attorney will help you avoid those difficulties, asking you practice questions that push your buttons.

PEOPLE BELIEVE WHAT OTHERS SAY ABOUT YOU

Rallying friends and family members to come to court and say good things about you can be the most difficult aspect of the process. But this testimony can be the most compelling and important, other than what you say yourself. It is essential that you do well on the stand, make a good impression and come across as someone reasonable. But if someone else takes the time and risks alienating your spouse to make a point in your favor, that can have a profound effect on the proceedings.

The truth is that while a judge or jury may like you and what you say, they may need the affirmation of others. No one believes what you say about yourself as much as they value the opinion of people close to you.

If you are trying to establish claims such as abuse or neglect of children or an addiction to drugs or gambling, the testimony of those who know you and your spouse will be essential. Without that, it becomes an exercise in "he said, she said."

Sometimes people are reluctant to testify because they feel the skeletons in their closet might come out to haunt them. That's when people need to understand how little attention the opposing attorney can afford to give most witnesses. If the person you want to speak for you is a convicted felon or a known drug kingpin, he or she may not be the best person to ask. But let's say that a minor character witness was married two decades ago and failed to pay child support, or engaged in questionable business dealings that could not possibly be known to your spouse. The chances of that being brought up in court are slim to none and shouldn't hurt your case even if it is known.

Work with your attorney to decide who will testify for you and what questions they will be asked. Your lawyer will know who will help you and who is either extraneous or dangerous to your case. For instance, a man might call a female co-worker to the stand to verify that he left work at a certain time each day and picked up his children at day care. But if the man and the woman employee had mad, passionate sex each day before he left for the day-care center, he might not want to bring these facts to light.

You may not want to ask a person to come to court for you, especially if that person knows your soon-to-be ex-spouse and the testimony could damage a relationship. But if your attorney feels that person is essential to your case, you must persuade him or her to testify.

CRUCIAL TIME: THE NIGHT BEFORE TRIAL

You've done your homework, answered all the questions you can, consulted with your attorney and advised others. Now is the time to rest and rejuvenate your mind and body for the task at hand.

You must overcome the sleepless nights that are common in contested divorces, especially divorces involving huge amounts of property or the custody of children. Try to take your mind off the proceedings the night before. Go to a movie or take in a sporting event. Don't succumb to pressure. Whatever happens the next day, your life will go on. It will go on more or less productively than ever, but you can bet your mind will be clear once again.

WHO HEARS FAMILY LAW CASES?

The system of family or domestic relations courts varies throughout the South. In many large cities of the region, certain courts are designated only as family courts. Lawyers with experience in family law are often either appointed or elected (depending on the laws of the particular state) to be judges in these courts. Similarly-trained attorneys often serve as special masters or assistant judges to hear motions or conduct preliminary hearings in these cases. Family courts hear divorces, child custody disputes and post-divorce modifications of divorce decrees. Sometimes, they certify adoptions or even hear juvenile cases and other matters not directly related to marriage and divorce.

Because judges and other court personnel in the family courts are usually experienced and educated in family law matters, you are most likely to have someone who understands your situation hear your case.

In other cities and small towns that do not have family law courts, those kinds of understandings are not so certain. In most of the South, courts that serve the less populated areas are often state district or circuit courts that handle a variety of civil cases. A judge in these courts may start the week by hearing a business lawsuit, then a modification of child custody suit, then a landlord-tenant dispute. Because this judge's plate is so full with a wide variety of matters from different legal areas, it is difficult for him to remain as current with the law as the judge who hears only family law cases.

Family law cases comprise 40% to 50% of all civil cases in most states. The issues they address are important to our society. Some states have proposed to establish multi-county family courts where litigants would travel across the area to have their cases heard. Or they've thought about having a family court judge travel to various court locations within a district for the same purpose. But any expansion of the court system costs money, and most states are laboring under large shortfalls that must be covered before they attempt additional spending.

In family law, the national trend is to move these disputes outside the courtroom. Today, less than 10% of all cases ever make it to court. The vast majority of cases are settled either in mediation, the collaborative law process or in less-formal settlement discussions.

Figure 7:
State Court Systems for Determining
Family Law Matters

State	Statewide Family Court System	Family Court System in Selected Areas	Family Courts Planned or Pilot	No Family Court System At This Time
Alabama		X		
Arkansas			X	
Florida	X			
Georgia		X		
Kentucky		X		
Louisiana		X		
Mississippi				X
North Carolina			X	
Oklahoma		X		
South Carolina	X			
Tennessee				X
Texas		X		
Virginia				X

Source: Excerpted from Chart 10: State Court Systems for Determining Family Law Matters, Family Law Quarterly, Volume 35, No. 4, Winter 2002. Copyright 2002 by the American Bar Association and updated on the ABA website November 2003. Reprinted by Permission.

Be On Your Best Behavior

Minding your manners is a southern tradition. Minding them in court is a necessity. In fact, your courtroom demeanor is so important that most family law attorneys suggest you begin to embrace good behavior the moment you leave your house for the courthouse.

Who knows if that sudden incident of road rage might be aimed at the judge, or in those states that allow juries in these cases, a jury member. Being seen yelling obscenities at those you want supporting you is no way to success.

In fact, your day in court should begin as you ready yourself for the day. Think of yourself as being on stage, in the spotlight. For any court appearance, you should dress professionally. For men, that usually means a suit or slacks and sport coat, a white or pastel shirt and a tie. Women should wear a nice dress or suit. If you have questions about the appropriate wardrobe, check with your attorney.

First impressions are very important in a custody or marital dispute where a judge or jury is forced to evaluate your credibility.

Always present yourself in court in a mature and professional manner. Never act threatening, try to intimidate the participants or crack jokes. There have been many instances of threats or actual harm to one party in a divorce. Judges are increasingly sensitive to any hint of violence, and they will restrain or even jail the potential offender if they feel it's necessary.

You may be seething with anger inside, but keep cool and collected. Many cases have settled on the steps of the courthouse because a litigant was able to convince the other side that he or she was confident about going to trial.

GETTING INTO COURT IS A TRIUMPH

It bares repeating that almost one-half of all the civil cases involve some facet of family law. If even 10% of the cases fail to settle and make it to court, that's a lot of trial time for a limited number of judges. If your divorce case was filed just three or four months ago, chances are that some older cases will be ahead of you on the court's docket or calendar. Cases are often reset several times before they reach trial.

The most common way to postpone a trial is the continuance. Parties may ask for a continuance or postponement because they aren't ready for trial. An attorney or a litigant may have a scheduling conflict, something the judge may or may not take into consideration. Or the court may already be in trial on a case that takes longer than expected.

The party obligated to pay money to the other spouse after the divorce may try to continue the case indefinitely. That party may even use the other person's need for money as a stall, to force an unequal settlement. The delay needs to be factored into any decision surrounding settlement and whether the trial court's potential ruling could outweigh the expenses associated with the delay. Actually going to court may be a greater triumph for passive partners of very domineering spouses. Your spouse may not believe you will actually go against his or her wishes. Sometimes, it's necessary to show a spouse what to expect from a trial. It is a statement that could be beneficial to you in all your future dealings with your ex.

When Is Your Appearance Definite?

A court's docket is like an airplane that is constantly overbooked. Your case may be among 10 or 15 cases that are set on the same day, when the court may only be able to accommodate one or two cases. The parties and witnesses for each case on the docket fill the courtroom. The hallways outside the courtroom are often filled to capacity with litigants and their attorneys attempting to resolve their cases at the last possible moment.

The very intimidation of being in court pressures many people to settle before court convenes.

Court procedures usually demand that judges call their dockets first thing in the morning. This is merely a check on the status of each case. The attorneys may say they are ready for trial but would like time to talk settlement. They may request a continuance or ask to speak privately with the judge to discuss a particular issue that must be clarified before they can proceed. Some cases will settle and the attorneys will notify the clerk of the court to remove them from the docket.

From those cases ready for trial, the judge will determine which will be heard that day and on into the week. The case with the oldest filing date usually has priority.

Sometimes there are emergencies to address, such as a threat of domestic violence or possible theft of property. Often the judge will decide to hear a case based on the level of seriousness. There may be several serious issues on the docket, and the judge will pick the most immediate emergency that he has the time to hear.

Often a case will overlap from the previous day, and it is normal to finish that one before starting another. This may require the rescheduling of all other cases on the docket.

The system is always overbooked like this and your attorney can do nothing about it. You may wait from three months to two years to get on a docket. You and your attorney may prepare for trial and your witnesses take off work to be here, and your case may be rescheduled. This is just one of the uncertainties associated with litigation.

Depending on the judge, your attorney may be able to call the courthouse the day before you are scheduled in court to determine where you are on the docket and what kind of cases are set before you. Some judges will tell your lawyer that a trial is in progress or a more pressing case must be resolved. Other judges require you to be at the courthouse each time the case is set.

CALMLY TELL THE TRUTH

Once your case begins, remember that cleverness is never a good tactic on the witness stand. Neither is hostility or indifference. Remain focused on the issue at hand. Sit up straight and speak clearly and politely. The judge is evaluating your responses to determine if you are the mercurial person your spouse says you are. Do not be argumentative with the opposing attorney or answer questions in a sarcastic manner.

Be cool and allow your attorney to field the grenades the other side lobs toward you. The other lawyer wants to get you upset on the stand. Don't help him achieve his goal.

When the opposing attorney asks you questions, answer truthfully. Lying is never the right idea, and it's also impractical. Get caught and you will ruin your credibility in front of the trial judge. Once you answer the question as briefly as possible, don't say anything else. If you have concerns about how to answer certain questions, discuss these with your attorney before you get to court.

In most cases, your attorney will map out a specific plan for handling the case at trial, based on the information available and how he or she knows the judge will respond. That experience may cause your attorney to disregard some evidence or testimony that you consider valuable but the attorney knows is irrelevant or will not register well with the judge.

A television newsmagazine recently chronicled a real-life takeoff on the tragi-comic theatrical movie, *War of the Roses*, starring Michael Douglas and Kathleen Turner. In the movie, the two Rose family members fought to the death during an especially messy divorce. In this latest war, South Florida attorney Michael Rose and his beauty queen wife fought for almost a year over every facet of their lives together. In one courtroom scene, the wife's attorney began a scathing cross examination of the husband over his work habits and other peccadillos, when the judge stopped him.

"This is a no-fault state," she reminded him. She was only interested in the size of their estate and how much they needed for living expenses. The cross examination, designed to embarrass and annoy the man, came to an abrupt halt.

THE FINAL DOCUMENT

When your divorce is final, either through settlement or trial, the judge will sign a document known in most jurisdictions as a final decree or judgment of divorce. This document spells out the terms and conditions under which the parties are divorced. If you reach a settlement of the divorce, the decree usually contains a settlement agreement signed by the parties that makes it binding on everyone. If the case goes to court, the decree spells out the court's verdict in the trial.

In most states of the South, you can be held in contempt for not following the terms of your decree. So it's important for you to read and understand its terms and conditions.

Your lawyer can explain your rights and responsibilities under the law. Don't rely on your memory of things, because emotions are at such a high level during a trial or settlement negotiations that you could miss something such as an exact property distribution, terms of sale of the marital residence or precise visitation details. Keep your divorce decree safe and nearby, so you can refer to it in the future as questions arise.

*Don't go to divorce
court for justice.
Go simply for a conclusion.*

Anonymous southern divorce attorney

PART FIVE

Once Your Divorce Is Final

25

Enforcing Your Decree

Y ou may have your day in court, but few people are happy with the results of litigation. That includes those who believe they won. This is your one opportunity to portray yourself in a good light, and most likely the only time your fate will ever be determined by the legal system. If you come out believing that you, your attorney or the people you brought as witnesses simply blew it, changing the outcome is difficult.

APPEALS ARE DIFFICULT AND RARE

While it's important to prepare your case well and get what you deserve through settlement or trial, in a few cases you may have success with a motion for a new trial or an appeal to a higher court.

In the *War of the Roses* case cited in the previous chapter, the husband appealed the judge's order on the division of assets as well as the amount of attorney fees. This is a tactic employed in some jurisdictions to delay support payments from the payer to the party who needs the money. In this case, the appeal might have saved the husband some monthly alimony payments. The decree called for cash payments each month for several years or until the wife remarried. The wife did remarry soon after the divorce.

In some jurisdictions, either party can file a motion to set aside the decree and gain a new trial. Even though this is possible, common sense tells you this is not going to work very often. This motion usually is not successful unless the court failed to consider a material fact in evidence or the judge made a clear error. You are asking the trial judge to admit that he or she made a mistake and didn't correct it before the trial was over. If you are not successful with your motion, and you still want to continue the effort, you are forced into the appeal process.

Appealing your case to a higher civil court is a last-ditch effort, and most appeals fail. Where they are allowed, only certain issues can be appealed, and the standard of review for such an appeal is usually stringent. Most successful appeals in divorce cases deal with specific issues such as a trial judge not allowing an important witness to testify. It is usually a blatant situation, such as the judge not allowing your business appraiser to testify after hearing the other side's expert.

Appeals have become more commonplace in divorces nationwide due to the increasing complexity of our lives. With more mechanisms for social and financial interaction, there are more opportunities for reversible error and, therefore, chances for appeal.

Many issues exist today that were unheard of 20 years ago in social relationships (same sex, stepparents, grandparents raising grandchildren, artificial reproduction), our daily lives (internet infidelity, the erosion of inter-spousal immunity; that is, spouses allowed to sue one another) and our financial lives (stock options, retirement plans, golden parachutes). There is little guidance in the way of precedent.

To deal with the rising frustration of divorce litigants and the resulting increase in appellate action, some states have moved to limit appeals to the most egregious cases. In Georgia, for example, all domestic relations cases are handled by discretionary appeal. That means you have to apply to the court for permission to appeal a case. The applications are granted in less than 10% of all cases in which appeals are sought and less than half of the appeals considered are successful.

The pathway of an appeal in almost any jurisdiction is usually from the trial court to a court of civil appeals or the state supreme court. It's an expensive move that can cost more than the divorce itself. If you hire a different lawyer to handle the appeal than the one who handled the original trial, the new lawyer will have to spend many hours getting familiar with the facts of the case before anyone can write the appeal brief.

Because of the expense and the low probability of success, you shouldn't file an appeal just to prove a point, even if you are certain you are right. Relying on the appeal process to remedy an injustice is something you should attempt only when large assets or the lives of your children are at stake.

YOUR DECREE: GUIDELINE OR SET IN STONE?

Once you determine to live by this divorce decree, you and your ex must ascertain how flexible you will be with its provisions as your lives change and your children get older. Understand that every change your ex may request is not cause for alarm. At these junctures, you should ask the following:

• Is this change better for the children?
• Is it better for me, both in the short-term or the long-run?
• Could this be the basis for a later change that I don't want?

• Can I trust this person to do this unofficially, or do I need to have my attorney look at it?

Just as every marriage is a compact between two individuals with different needs and abilities, so is every divorce. There are no set rules for how much to give and when to put your foot down. You only have common sense and your history making decisions for your family to guide you.

Most people who successfully deal with divorce make lots of changes as the kids grow up. These people act in the best interest of their children, have few ego-driven clashes and truly want the best for everyone. Reaching this place can take time and patience.

Along the way, you may be one of those parents who are driven nearly insane because the ex was supposed to have the children back at 8 p.m. and here it's 8:10 and they aren't home. Could they be in a car wreck or did he kidnap them? But the truth is that people who are happily married are late, too, or forget about their mates and children altogether. People who love their kids get interested in something and lose track of time. The only advice I can give you in this divorced parent role is to relax and look at every situation on its own merits.

AN ANNUAL LEGAL CHECKUP COULD HELP

If you are continually plagued by feelings of mistrust for your ex, and it doesn't subside, perhaps a visit to your divorce attorney sometime after the divorce is final will help you sort through your feelings and decide what is reasonable and how prone you are to hysteria.

You often schedule refresher sessions with financial planners or therapists. You may not need or be able to afford regular, continuing sessions with these professionals, but an occasional conversation can be a good idea. If you arrange annual help sessions with your attorney, you can ask a variety of questions, including:

- Can we receive more (or pay less) child support because of changing financial circumstances?
- My ex wants more visitation with the children. What is fair?
- Must I (or should I) give my ex's parents visitation?
- If I have a great job offer out of state, should I take it?
- If I remarry, how will this affect my agreements with my ex?
- If I find out about assets my ex hid in the divorce, can I go back to court?

You have regular physical exams and tune up your car on a maintenance schedule, so why not check out your legal well-being, especially if you have children or continuing financial ties to your former spouse. For most people, these checkups can be valuable each year for the first couple of years and then become unnecessary as time goes along.

DON'T BE TOO GREEDY

There's an expression that pigs get fat while hogs get slaughtered. If everything must go totally your way and you never give an inch, you can cut off many of the good things that could come to you and your children through mutual agreement with your ex.

Here's an example: A man with two children agreed in the divorce to pay a generous amount of child support. Although he wasn't obligated to pay anything additional, he also picked up the cost of music lessons and tuition to a music camp for his kids, registered them for soccer and bought them clothing and uniforms.

When the man asked his ex-wife if they could occasionally extend his weekend visitation by allowing the children to sleep over on Sunday, she refused to consider it because it wasn't in their original agreement.

Under the laws of every state, child support is not tied to the amount of visitation the paying spouse can expect. But when the man took his request to court, his generosity took center stage. Besides providing more money for his children, he had allowed his ex-wife to use his lake house for a reunion of her family. He also stood by when she had a surgical procedure and needed extended help with the kids.

The point is that in many cases, reasonable, responsible people get special consideration in family court. He was granted the extra visitation over the objection of his former wife.

In the family courts of most southern states, reason and generosity often give you brownie points that you can cash in when necessary. Those virtues also provide a good lesson for your children and can make the long-term relationship with your ex more productive.

WHEN CONTEMPT CITATIONS ARE NECESSARY

When one party to a divorce simply won't comply with the law, a court can hold that person in contempt. Contempt is used to enforce many different orders in your divorce decree. One party must willfully refuse to comply with a specific order of the court that is central to the obligation in question. For example, if one party owes child support and refuses to pay it, even though he has the means to do so, judges in many locales would hold him in contempt.

In a contempt action, you ask the court to put the offender in jail or impose a fine for failure to comply. Sometimes, this drastic action is necessary to show the offending party that what the judge ordered isn't just a suggestion of the action to take.

Of course, it may not be contempt if the other side simply does not have the money. Jail time is serious, and you must weigh the seriousness of the contempt against the reality of jailing the mother or father of your children. Under a contempt action, a party may be placed in jail for the contempt and released by satisfying the judge. If unpaid child support brought on the contempt action, paying back support will purge the contempt. If the party is financially unable to pay, the court may not keep that person in jail. But in many cases, relatives or new spouses come forward to pay the amount due.

26

Modifying Your Decree After the Fact

O nce your divorce case is over, chances are that you'll never want to see another courtroom or speak to another attorney ever again. Divorces can drain the joy from your life, and in most cases you will want to get on with living.

In some instances, though, circumstances arise that require you to revisit the case. This is different from an appeal, for you may need to modify your decree or fight off efforts by your ex to change the terms of your divorce.

The most common modifications are child custody, child support and visitation. If you find where your spouse hid the family treasure during the divorce, you might want to go back and recover your share. And in some southern states, some issues can be held in reserve, well after the divorce is final, and may need to be reexamined by the judge to make sure they are fair.

To seek a modification, you must prove that a basic change has taken place since the last court hearing. That change must be important enough to demand a new look at the terms of the divorce.

AN INTENSE CUSTODY TRIAL

Most southern states recognize joint custody as the preferred parenting option. This custody arrangement is an attempt to equalize the rights and responsibilities of the two parents. But joint custody does not necessarily mean equal time with the children, so conflicts arise over the role of parents in this and other types of custody arrangements. Sometimes these conflicts become so severe that a parent gets frustrated and decides to sue to change the custody arrangement.

A full-blown custody trial is the most extreme example of an attempted divorce decree modification. The parent asking for this modification can't just say that he or she really, really wants custody of the children. That party must show that a material change of circumstances has occurred that makes the court order unworkable and that changing the custody arrangement would be a positive improvement for the child. The burden of proving the allegations differs by jurisdiction and depends on the circumstances of the arrangement in place.

As we discussed earlier, this fight is not for the faint at heart. Just mention the words "custody battle" and distinct lines are drawn. Your friends and family members begin to take sides, and you will need to ask some of them to testify if the case gets to court.

You must decide whether all of this is worth it. Has your child been harmed or are you just upset? If your ex remarries or has a new relationship, does this mean your child's situation is worse? Parents sometimes demonize the ex's new partner so badly in the child's eyes that the child feels he or she is being harmed. It is a particularly devious form of child abuse that can backfire on the parent seeking revenge.

But what if the parent and that new partner engage in sex in front of the child? What if there are provable signs of physical abuse, drug abuse or other criminal conduct, undue mental pressure on the child or neglect? What if one parent is often intoxicated and endangers the child by driving drunk with the child in the car?

The court that hears your case wants to ascertain what is in the best interest of the *child*, not the parents. In determining whether to modify custody, the court may look at a number of factors, including:

- Overall performance of the child at home and in school
- Desires of the child (the importance of this depends on the child's age and maturity level)
- The child's activities and friends
- Parents' relative stability and home life
- Parents' ability to provide for the child both in economic resources and time
- Parents' travel schedules

If a parent who has the child during the week is unable to get the child to school on time, it makes sense to determine if the other parent is better able to perform that function. If the parent with custody avoids living near families with children and the other parent loves to have kids in the house, maybe some alteration in custody is warranted.

Just having more money than your ex doesn't necessarily give you an advantage in a custody battle. Most state laws don't favor living in a million-dollar mansion over being raised in a mobile home.

If you file for custody, be prepared to have your life examined closely. Most urban counties have at least one counselor who studies the parties and their households in these cases to determine their fitness, and reports their findings to the court.

Many custody cases are settled out of court. Settlements take place when you get what you want or when you realize that you can't accomplish everything you would like. Because changes of custody are so difficult, many people are upset to find that they may not be able to change the conditions in which their children are living.

Joint custody and mediation have cut down on the number of full-blown custody trials, but they still take place when people confront an intractable issue or one parent or the other decides to play hardball with the system. Sometimes the way you approach the original trial affects the outcome of the later trial for modification. It is shocking how many parents agree to give an abusive parent either joint custody or substantial visitation rights with a child that parent has abused during the marriage. Later, it is difficult to convince a trial judge during a modification proceeding that the other parent's access should be limited when you've granted that parent expanded visitation even after you knew abuse took place.

Custody trials are street battles that divide entire families and sets of friends. They cost enormous amounts of money in fees for attorneys and expert witnesses. They involve the lives of parents, children, friends and associates being examined for their suitability as parents and people. Family law involves more emotion and tension than any other area of the law, and the trial to modify custody is one of the most tension-filled and emotional actions of all.

But winning a modification of child custody can be the most rewarding of all parental actions, if your child's quality of life is at stake. Before you decide to take such a course, think about the following:

- How will this action affect your child?
- How will it affect you and other family members?
- Can you count on friends and family members to help you with this, including testifying in court if necessary?
- Are you prepared to invest the time and money necessary to accomplish this?

• Can you afford it?

• What is the best outcome you can reasonably expect and what's the downside of taking action?

• What will happen if you don't pursue this action?

These are questions you and your attorney should discuss before making a decision to seek a change in custody.

A QUESTION OF CHILD SUPPORT

A financial windfall for either party, after the divorce is over, should benefit the children of divorce as much as if the family remained intact. Kids get new bicycles and larger rooms in fancier houses when the parents make more money. Increases or decreases in the income of either party influence modifications to prior child support awards.

If the income of either spouse has increased or decreased significantly, the child support amount should be adjusted.

Both parents have a duty to support their children the best they can. Your ex may pay for expenses and activities over and above the mandated child support obligation. You may not want to risk having those extra payments discontinued by fighting for a slight increase in child support. Every state has adopted some form of child support guidelines. Most divorce experts can calculate the projected new child support payment under your facts, provided you have income figures for both parents. In that way, you can determine if those extra payments equal or exceed the amount you would get if you took the matter back to court.

Sometimes parents obligated to pay child support take defensive actions when called on to pay more. For example, a parent without custody may attempt to seek custody when the child support modification action is filed. This action may be apparent to the court as an effort to avoid paying higher child support, but it can create considerable problems and expense for the custodial parent who is seeking an increase in child support.

If you have had less than exemplary conduct since the divorce, you may not want to ask for a modification of child support because custody could come into question. The fact that you are living with a friend of the opposite sex may not seem like a big deal to you. But it can cloud the issue of child support and lead to a counter-petition by the other parent for custody of the children.

For every action in family court, there is an equal and opposite reaction. Modifications give rise to many reactions that people may have never considered in advance.

MODIFYING VISITATION

Good parents are, in most cases, entitled to have as much access to their children as possible. After the heat of divorce has cooled, many parents control kids' schedules between themselves. Informal modifications are common, but they aren't enforceable by law. Most parents find that as their children get older, everyone needs a little flexibility. This cooperation is recommended, as long as you feel comfortable with the changes and the fact that they are not mandated by the courts.

Quite often, those changes involve a visiting parent getting more time with the children. A teenage child may want to take a long trip with that parent or spend an entire summer with the grandparents. Some changes are brought about by refinements in the visitation guidelines. For instance, some parents who would otherwise take the children home on a Sunday night after a weekend visitation now keep the children Sunday night and take them to school the next morning. Each request should be carefully considered by the custodial parent, keeping in mind the needs of the child, the ability of the other parent to accept this responsibility and how the changes may affect your future rights.

Visitation changes are often mediated by the social workers in family court services, after interviewing parents and sometimes seeking information from friends and family members.

These modifications, like all others, are expensive to achieve if you have to go to court. You might spend several thousand dollars to get one additional evening of visitation or deny your ex that amount of time with your children. Remember, your children invariably get older and circumstances change. If you and your ex-spouse can remain flexible and reasonable, you can avoid a lot of heartache down the road.

OTHER CHANGES

Occasionally, one party to a divorce has been known to hide a piece of property so that it will not become part of the divorce settlement. In some jurisdictions, if the other party is able to locate the property, he or she can petition the court to reopen the case and take the found property into consideration in the total settlement.

If certain kinds of fraud take place during the divorce and are not discovered until after the divorce is final, some trial court judges can set aside the division of property. How long you have to bring such a cause of action can vary depending on where it happened and the facts of the case. Ask your attorney if such remedies are available in your state.

27

Achieving Successful Divorce in the South

So here is the good news; though a great number of people are divorcing in the South, the totals seem to be flattening out and may actually be declining. The concerted effort to identify the problem and solve it over the past few years may be working. You cannot pass the marquee in front of a southern church these days without reading about a divorce support or recovery class. In some age groups, there seems to be a cultural shift away from splitting up on a whim and toward working things out and staying together.

But there will always be the bad news; for those who divorce in the South, the reality is all too painful. You are hurt and angry, confused and stunned. No one has ever felt this bad. You think of yourself as powerless, friendless, without joy. You are facing divorce, and divorce is just no fun — not for you, your children, your family or your friends.

At precisely the moment you feel the worst, you must decide what kind of divorce you will have. You can remain a victim, allowing yourself to be pushed around. You can decide to become a vindictive person, extracting your vengeance on everyone involved. Or you can decide that this will be a different kind of divorce. That kids can be kids, without having to take on unnecessary baggage. That divorcing parties will act like adults instead of adolescents. Out of all this can come a brighter future for people with greater stability and maturity. You can emerge financially and emotionally whole.

SUCCESSFUL DIVORCE PRINCIPLES

It is at this time that you should embrace the successful divorce by following these principles:

• Decide if divorce really is the answer for you.
• Look for resolution, not revenge.
• Don't confuse what's best for the children with what satisfies your vengeful side.
• Hire the most experienced family law attorney you can afford and one who matches your personality.
• Try to keep your divorce uncontested.
• Mediate in good faith.
• Stockpile useful family information.
• Be truthful with your attorney.
• Decide who gets which assets between you and your spouse.
• Don't let a court decide for you, if possible.
• Decide what's in the best interest of your children and follow that path.
• Don't be too greedy.
• If your spouse concedes something he or she doesn't have to, be grateful.
• If mediation fails, get ready for trial.

- Present yourself well before the judge or jury.
- Remember that if you don't get everything you want,
  your life will continue.
- Consider this: Will this divorce settlement leave you and
  your family in a good situation, whether you remarry or not.

Divorce is a mixed bag of complex issues. You have to look at the way your life is today, tomorrow and into the future. The settlement agreement attempts to address every possible issue you can imagine in the future, but it cannot. Remember that if you and your spouse have not been able to agree during the marriage, you probably will not be able to agree on very much after the divorce.

When you are in the midst of a divorce, the last thing you want to consider is getting married again. But statistics tell us that well over half the people who get divorced for the first time will remarry. Your chances for happiness are narrowed considerably if you leave yourself financially wounded and with a difficult custody arrangement. Bad agreements can make remarriage too costly and a full life nearly impossible.

The only way to avoid such a tragedy is to consult with an expert in matrimonial law in your area before proceeding with a divorce action. Do not execute any documents without the advice and approval of an attorney. Furthermore, do not rely on the advice of friends, family or your spouse's attorney when determining what is an appropriate settlement. Your spouse's attorney cannot advise you about your actions; his sole purpose is to protect his client, your spouse.

No Matter Where You Live in the South, Know Your Divorce Laws

Regrettably, everyone you talk to is an expert in divorce. They all have a cousin who got a divorce somewhere, and they will let you know that you need to do what they did. Listen politely, then consult with someone who knows the law. As we have shown in this book, it's not enough just to know family law in general. The rules vary in each southern state we are discussing. Your best advisor is a respected family law specialist in your state.

It is likely that your divorce will be one of the most difficult issues you will have to deal with during your lifetime. Be prepared to go into battle and perfectly able to avoid the war. By doing so, you can prevent a bad situation from becoming an impossible one.

Appendix A
Glossary of Family Law Terms

-A-

ACTION: A lawsuit or proceeding in a court of law.

AFFIDAVIT: A written statement under oath.

AGREEMENT: A verbal or written resolution of disputed issues.

ANSWER: The written response to a complaint, petition or motion.

ALIENATION OF AFFECTION: Also called a "heart balm" case, a lawsuit that contends a third party unlawfully took away the love of a spouse.

ALIMONY: A payment of support provided by one spouse to the other.

ANNULMENT: The marriage is declared void, as though it never took place.

APPEAL: A legal action where the losing party requests that a higher court review the decision.

ASSET: Everything owned by you or your spouse, including property, cars, furniture, bank accounts, jewelry, life insurance policies, businesses, or retirement plans.

ATTORNEY: A person with special education and training in the field of law. Only an attorney is allowed to give you legal advice. In family law matters, you are not entitled to a court-appointed lawyer, like a public defender in a criminal case. However, legal assistance is often available for those who are unable to hire a private attorney.

-B-

BILLING: An accounting of hours spent on your case by the attorney, his legal assistant and others. Usually calculated monthly.

-C-

CERTIFIED MAIL: Mail that requires the receiving party to sign as proof of receipt.

CHILD SUPPORT: Money paid from one parent to the other for the benefit of their dependent or minor children.

CHILD SUPPORT GUIDELINES: Each state has child support guidelines that must be followed in awarding child support. The guidelines are a formula. There are only a few circumstances when the court can award child support higher or lower than the guidelines.

CLOSELY HELD BUSINESS: A business that is privately owned, such as a family business.

COMPLAINANT: The one who files the suit, same as plaintiff.

COMMON LAW MARRIAGE: A common law marriage comes about when a man and woman who are free to marry agree to live together as husband and wife without the formal ceremony. To be married under common law, both spouses must have intended to be husband and wife.

COMMUNITY PROPERTY: Term used in 10 states to denote property that belongs of both parties to the marriage.

CONTEMPT: Failure to follow a court order. One side can request that the court determine that the other side is in contempt and punish him or her.

CONTINGENCY FEE: When attorneys are paid on recovery of assets in a lawsuit. This is illegal in family law cases in most states.

CONTINUANCE: Postponement of a trial or hearing.

CONTESTED ISSUES: Any or all issues upon which the parties are unable to agree and which must be resolved by the judge at a hearing or trial.

CONTINGENT ASSET: In some jurisdictions, an asset that you may receive or get later, such as income, tax refund, accrued vacation or sick leave, a bonus, or an inheritance.

CONTINGENT LIABILITY: In some jurisdictions, a liability that you may owe later, such as payments for lawsuits, unpaid taxes, or debts that you have agreed or guaranteed to pay if someone else does not.

CORROBORATING WITNESS: A person who testifies for you and backs up your story. If you are asking the court to grant a divorce or custody of a child, you should bring to court a witness who can corroborate your grounds for divorce or a basis for having custody.

COUNTERPETITION: A written request to the court for legal action, which is filed by a respondent after being served with a petition.

COVENANT MARRIAGE: Requires fault to be assessed before a divorce can be granted. More difficult to dissolve than regular marriages.

CUSTODIAL: Dealing with child custody; usually denotes the parent with custody.

CUSTODY-SOLE & JOINT: Refers to the legal arrangements for whom a child will live with and how decisions about the child will be made. Custody has two parts: legal and physical. Legal custody is the decision-making part: physical custody refers to where the child lives on a regular basis. Generally, the parent the child does not live with will be allowed to have regular visits with the child. The standard for custody is "best interest of the child."

-D-

DEFAULT: A party's failure to answer a complaint, motion or petition.

DEFENDANT: The person the case is brought against.

DELINQUENT: Late.

DEPOSITION: Discovery in which an attorney asks questions of the opposing party under oath.

DOCKET: A court's calendar of cases.

DISCOVERY: A way of getting information from the other side or other people. Examples are interrogatories (written questions) and depositions (questions which are usually in person and recorded).

DISSOLUTION: The legal end of a marriage.

-E-

ENJOINED: Prohibited by the court from doing a specific act.

EQUITABLE DIVISION: The method of dividing property in a divorce used in most states; involves dividing property fairly, based on a number of factors.

EX PARTE: Communication with the judge by only one party. In order for a judge to speak with either party, the other party must have been properly notified and have an opportunity to be heard.

-F -

FILING: Giving the court clerk your legal papers.

FILING FEE: An amount of money, set by law, that the petitioner must pay when filing a case.

FINAL HEARING: Trial in your case.

FINANCIAL AFFIDAVIT: A sworn statement that contains information regarding your income, expenses, assets and liabilities.

FINAL JUDGMENT: A written document signed by a judge and recorded in the clerk of the circuit court's office that contains the judge's decision in your case.

FORENSIC AUDIT: An audit or appraisal of assets for the purpose of offering testimony on its value.

-G-

GROUNDS FOR DIVORCE: The legal basis for a divorce; the law sets out specific reasons for a divorce to be proven before the divorce is granted.

GUARDIAN AD LITEM: A neutral person who may be appointed by the court to evaluate or investigate your child's situation, and file a report with the court about what is in the best interests of children.

-H-

HEARING: A legal proceeding before a judge or designated officer (general master or hearing officer) on a motion.

-I-

INTERROGATORIES: Written questions submitted to each party in a divorce.

-J-

JUDGE: An official who is responsible for deciding matters on which you and the other parties in your case are unable to agree. A judge is a neutral person responsible for ensuring that your case is resolved in a fair, equitable, and legal manner.

JUDGMENT: A court's decision.

JURISDICTION: The authority of the court to hear a case.

-K-

-L-

LIABILITIES: Everything owed by you or your spouse, including mortgages, credit cards or car loans.

LUMP SUM ALIMONY: Money to be paid by one spouse to another in a limited number of payments, often a single payment.

-M-

MARITAL ASSET: Generally, anything that you and/or your spouse acquired or received (by gift or purchase) during the marriage. For example, something you owned before your marriage may be non-marital.

MARITAL LIABILITY: Generally, any debt that you and/or your spouse incurred during the marriage.

MARITAL RESIDENCE: The family home.

MEDIATOR: A person trained and certified to assist parties in reaching an agreement before going to court. Mediators do not take either party's side and are not allowed to give legal advice. They are only responsible for helping the parties reach an agreement and putting that agreement into writing. In some areas, mediation of certain family law cases is required before going to court.

MODIFICATION: A change made by the court in an order or final judgment.

MOTION: A request made to the court, other than a petition.

MARITAL PROPERTY: Includes all property acquired during the marriage, even if it is not titled in both names, with some exceptions.

MASTER: Hears cases like a judge. A master's decision is reviewed by a judge before becoming final.

-N-

NO-FAULT: A type of divorce in which the divorcing parties don't need to state specific reasons for the divorce, other than irreconcilable differences.

NONCUSTODIAL: Pertaining to the parent without custody of the children.

NONMARITAL ASSET: Generally, anything owned separately by you or your spouse.

NONMARITAL LIABILITY: Generally, any debt that you or your spouse incurred before your marriage or since your separation.

NOTARY PUBLIC: A person authorized to witness signatures on court-related forms.

-O-

OBLIGEE: A person to whom money, such as child support or alimony, is owed.

OBLIGOR: A person who is ordered by the court to pay money, such as child support or alimony.

ORDER: A written decision signed by a judge and filed in the clerk of court's office, that contains the judge's decision on part of your case, usually on a motion.

-P-

PARENTING COURSE: Teaches parents how to help their children cope with divorce and other family issues.

PARTY: A person involved in a court case, either as a petitioner or respondent.

PATERNITY ACTION: A lawsuit used to determine whether a designated individual is the father of a specific child or children.

PAYER: An employer or other person who provides income to an obligor.

PENDENTE LITE: Temporary arrangements for custody, child support, child visitation, alimony, possession of the family home, etc., until a final hearing.

PERMANENT ALIMONY: Spousal support ordered to be paid at a specified, periodic rate until modified by a court order, the death of either party, or the remarriage of the obligee, whichever occurs first.

PERSONAL SERVICE: When a summons and a copy of a petition (or other pleading) that has been filed with the court are delivered by a deputy sheriff or private process server to the other party. Personal service is required for all petitions and supplemental petitions.

PETITIONER: The person who files the legal paper that begins a court case.

PLAINTIFF: The person who starts the case.

PLEADING: A formal written statement of exactly what a party wants the court to do in a lawsuit or court action.

PRENUPTIAL AGREEMENT: Also called a "prenup," is an agreement for the division of assets if the parties should divorce.

PRIMARY RESIDENCE: The home in which the children spends most of their time.

PROCESS SERVER: Person who serves legal papers on those being sued.

PRO SE: Representing yourself in court without an attorney.

PRO SE LITIGANT: A person who appears in court without the assistance of a lawyer.

-Q-

QDRO: Called a Quadro, is a planned division of a retirement account.

-R-

RECONCILIATION: Married people about to divorce getting back together.

REHABILITATIVE ALIMONY: Spousal support ordered to be paid for a limited period of time to allow one of the parties an opportunity to complete a plan of education or training, according to a rehabilitative plan accepted by the court, so that he or she may better support himself or herself.

RESPONDENT: The person who is served with a petition requesting some legal action against him or her.

-S-

SCIENTIFIC PATERNITY TESTING: A medical test to determine who is the father of a child.

SERVICE: Providing a copy of the papers being filed to the other side.

SETTLEMENT AGREEMENT: A document that sets out agreement between the two parties when a divorce is settled.

SPOUSE: Husband or wife.

SUBPOENA: A form issued by the court requiring someone to appear in court and/or bring documents.

SUPERVISED VISITATION: A parenting arrangement under which visitation between a parent and his or her children is supervised by either a friend, family member or a supervised visitation center, usually for the protection of the children.

SUPPLEMENTAL PETITION: A petition that may be filed by either party after the judge has made a decision in a case and a final judgment or order has been entered. For example, a supplemental petition may be used to request that the court modify the previously entered final judgment or order.

-T-

TRIAL: The final hearing in a contested case.

-U-

UNCONTESTED DIVORCE: When the defendant is not going to try to stop the divorce and there are no issues for the court to decide about the children, money or property.

-V-

VALUE BILLING: When the amount of attorney fees is based on hourly rate and final results.

VENUE: The jurisdiction where the case is heard.

VISITATION: The time that the parent that does not have primary residence spends with the children.

-W-

WRIT OF SUMMONS: A form issued by the court directing a party to respond to a complaint, motion or petition.

APPENDIX B
CHILD SUPPORT ENFORCEMENT
IN THE SOUTH

Alabama Department of Human Resources
Child Support Enforcement Division
P.O. Box 304000
Montgomery, AL 36130-4000
334/242-9300
334/242-0606 fax
www.dhr.state.al.us/csed/default.asp

Arkansas Department of Finance and Administration
1/800/264-2445
www.state.ar.us/dfa/childsupport/index.html

Florida Child Support Enforcement
1/800/622-KIDS (5437)
sun6.dms.state.fl.us/dor/childsupport/

Georgia Child Support Enforcement
404/657-2780 (area codes 404,678,770 and outside GA)
1/800/227-7993 (area codes 229, 478, 706, 912)
www.cse.dhr.state.ga.us/

Commonwealth of Kentucky
Office of the Attorney General
Child Support Enforcement Commission
The Capitol, Suite 118

700 Capitol Ave.

Frankfort, KY 40601-3449

502/696-5300

502/564-2894 fax

www.law.state.ky.us/childsupport/Default.htm

Louisiana Department of Social Services

New Orleans Regional Support Enforcement Services Office

2235 Poydras

New Orleans, LA 70153-3446

504/826-2269

(Serves the parishes of Orleans, Plaquemines and St. Bernard. Other regional offices serve other parishes in the state.)

www.dss.state.la.us/

North Carolina Division of Social Services

1/800/992-9457

www.ncchildsupport.com

Oklahoma Child Support Enforcement Division

Oklahoma Department of Human Services

P.O. Box 53552

Oklahoma City, OK 73152

1/800/522-2922

www.okdhs.org/childsupport/

South Carolina Child Support Enforcement

S.C. Department of Social Services

P.O. Box 1469

Columbia, SC 29202-1469

1/800/768-5858

www.state.sc.us/dss/csed/

Tennessee Department of Human Services

1/800/838-6911

615/253-4394 (in Nashville)

www.state.tn.us/humanserv/child_support.htm#contact

State of Texas

Office of the Attorney General

Child Support Program

1/800/252-8014

www.oag.state.tx.us/child/mainchil.htm

Virginia Department of Social Services

730 E. Broad St.

Richmond, VA 23219

804/692-1900

www.dss.state.va.us/family/dcse.html

APPENDIX C
JOINT LEGAL AND PHYSICAL CUSTODY
(SAMPLE LANGUAGE)

A. The children's primary residence shall be with Wife. Husband shall have custodial time with the minor children for such periods of time as the parties shall mutually agree. Both parties agree that the children's wishes and scheduled activities shall be considered when scheduling custodial time. In the event the parties are unable to agree with regard to Husband's custodial time, the following terms will govern:

(a)(1)   <u>Weekends</u>: Every other weekend commencing Friday at 6 PM until 6 PM on Sunday.

(a)(2)   <u>Weekdays</u>: Every Wednesday commencing at 5 PM until Husband returns the children to Wife's residence or school by 8 AM the following Thursday morning.

(b)   <u>Holiday Schedule</u>: The following holiday schedule shall take priority over the regular schedule set forth in subsections (a)(1) and (2) in the event of any conflict.

(b)(1)   <u>Martin Luther King Day</u>: Husband shall have custodial time with the minor children in all even numbered years commencing at the time school adjourns on the Friday preceding Martin Luther King Day until 5 PM on Martin Luther King Day. Wife shall have custodial time with the minor children in all odd numbered years for the same time period.

(b)(2)   <u>Spring Break</u>: In all odd numbered years, Husband shall have custodial time with the minor children on each of their respective spring breaks commencing at the time school adjourns on the Friday prior to the week of spring break for each respective child and extending until Husband returns the minor child or children to Wife's residence at 5 PM the Sunday before school resumes following spring break. Wife shall have custodial time with the minor children on each such respective child's spring break in even numbered years during the same time period.

(b)(3) Easter Holiday: Wife shall have custodial time with the minor children on odd numbered years and Husband on even numbered years. The Easter Holiday custodial time shall begin when the children are let out of school prior to Easter Sunday and continue through 5 PM on the day before school resumes following Easter Sunday. In the event the Easter holiday as described in this paragraph falls on a child's spring break, the spring break schedule as described herein shall take precedence.

(b)(4) Mother's Day: Wife shall have custodial time with the minor children the weekend of Mother's Day irrespective of the weekend schedule otherwise described herein.

(b)(5) Father's Day: Husband shall have custodial time with the minor children the weekend of Father's Day, commencing at the time school adjourns on the Friday preceding Father's Day to 5 PM Father's Day.

(b)(6) Memorial Day Holiday: Husband shall have custodial time with the minor children in all odd numbered years commencing at the time school adjourns on the Friday preceding Memorial Day until 5 PM on Memorial Day. Wife shall have custodial time with the minor children in all even numbered years for the same time period.

(b)(7) Labor Day Holiday: Husband shall have custodial time with the minor children in all even numbered years commencing at the time school adjourns on the Friday preceding Labor Day until 5 PM on Labor Day. Wife shall have custodial time with the minor children in all odd numbered years for the same time period.

(b)(8) Thanksgiving Holiday: In all odd numbered years, Husband shall have custodial time with the minor children commencing at the time school adjourns on the Wednesday preceding Thanksgiving until 5 PM on the Sunday following Thanksgiving. Wife shall have custodial time with the minor children for the same time period in all even numbered years.

(b)(9) Christmas Holiday: In all even numbered years Husband shall have custodial time with the minor children commencing at the time school adjourns for the Christmas break until 6 PM on December 26, and in odd numbered years from 6 PM on December 26th through 5 PM on January 1st. In odd numbered years, Wife shall have custodial time with the minor children commencing at the time school adjourns for the Christmas break through 6 PM on December 26, and in even numbered years from 6 PM on December 26th until school resumes following the Christmas break.

(b)(10) Summer Visitation: Husband shall have two (2) uninterrupted consecutive weeks or two (2) non-consecutive weeks of custodial time with the minor children during the summer months. Wife shall have the same summer vacation privileges with the minor children, i.e. two (2) uninterrupted consecutive weeks or two (2) non-consecutive weeks. The parties shall provide the other party ninety (90) days written notice of the two weeks in which he or she wishes to exercise his or her vacation time. If there is a conflict with the weeks so chosen by Husband, his choice shall prevail in odd numbered years and Wife's choice shall prevail in all even numbered years. Any summer camps that have been previously agreed upon by both parents will have priority over the vacation schedule.

B. Husband and the minor children will have the right to communicate with each other over the telephone and internet at any reasonable time and for reasonable periods of time. Wife shall have the same rights when the minor children are with Husband.

C. Each party agrees to provide the other party the telephone number, address and flight information of the children when that party travels with the children outside the area. Further, each party shall promptly notify the other of any illness or accident or other circumstances effecting a child or the children's health or general welfare.

D. In the event of any change of residence on the part of either party herein so long as the children are minors, said party changing his or her residence shall notify the other party at least one (1) month in advance of any change of residence and of the location of the new residence and shall furnish to him or her the complete new address and, as soon as determined, the new telephone number at the new residence.

E. Each parent shall be entitled to complete, detailed information from any pediatrician, general physician, dentist, consultant or specialist attending the children for any reason whatsoever and to be furnished with copies of any reports given by them or any of them to the other party. Each parent shall be entitled to consult with all such care providers.

F. Each parent shall be entitled to complete, detailed information from any teacher or school giving instruction to a child, or which the children may attend, and to be furnished with copies of all reports given by them and any of them to the other parent; each party shall have the right to notify the school of his or her desire for information and notice. Further, both parties shall have the right to be in attendance at any teacher conferences or counseling sessions or meetings involving the children.

G. Each parent shall have the right to attend the children's sporting events and extracurricular activities, or any other events parents normally participate as spectators. The parent having knowledge of the scheduled events shall provide notice to the other parent so he or she can attend if so desired.

H. This Agreement cannot provide for every possible detail with respect to custody and visitation; the parties agree that strict compliance with time and schedules set forth herein will not always be possible and agree that substantial compliance will be adequate.

NOTES:

NOTES:

NOTES:

NOTES:

KF535.Z9 M29 2004 Burke

Mayoue, John C., 1954-
Southern divorce

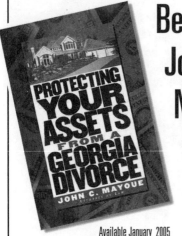

Available January 2005

Be Sure to Pick Up
John C. Mayoue's
New Book on the
Financial Aspects
Of Divorce in Georgia

ONE OF MANY FINE
LEGAL GUIDES
FROM PSG BOOKS

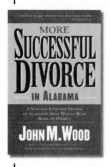

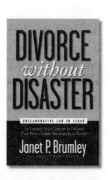

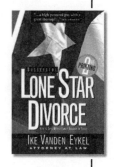

PSG Books publishes the work of outstanding legal talents across the country in state-specific guides for people facing divorce. These volumes are available at your local book-seller, online at Amazon.com or bn.com or by calling Independent Publishers Group at

1/800/888-4741